YOU'RE ONLY YOUNG TWICE!

for Peter Campbell
with thanks
for his help with
this book, as
with several
others...

First published in France in 2007 by Gallimard Jeunesse.
First published in Great Britain in 2008 by Andersen Press Ltd.,
20 Vauxhall Bridge Road, London SW1V 2SA.
Published in Australia by Random House Australia Pty.,
Level 3, 100 Pacific Highway, North Sydney, NSW 2060.
Copyright © Quentin Blake, 2007.
The rights of Quentin Blake to be identified
as the author and illustrator of this work have
been asserted by him in accordance with the
Copyright, Designs and Patents Act, 1988.
All rights reserved.
Printed and bound in Malaysia.

ISBN 978 1 84270 856 9

4   5   6   7   8   9   10

British Library Cataloguing in Publication Data available.

Quentin Blake

YOU'RE ONLY YOUNG TWICE!

ANDERSEN PRESS

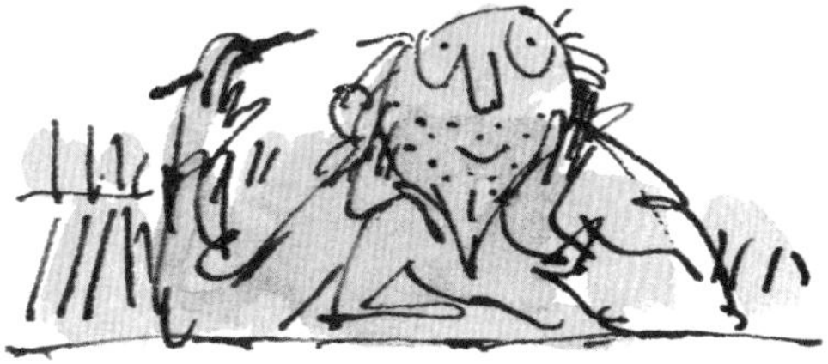

Of the three hundred or so books I have illustrated at least three quarters must have been for children – even though they have things in them which I hope will speak to adults too. But this is the first time that I have found myself at work on a book specifically for my contemporaries: if it had a guide to age suitability on it, as some children's books do, it would have to say: "60 and up."

The first step in the direction of this book was taken a couple of years ago when I was invited to produce a set of pictures to decorate the walls of a residential wing for elderly patients in a London hospital. The idea of my characters finding themselves in trees, and even swinging from branch to branch, came

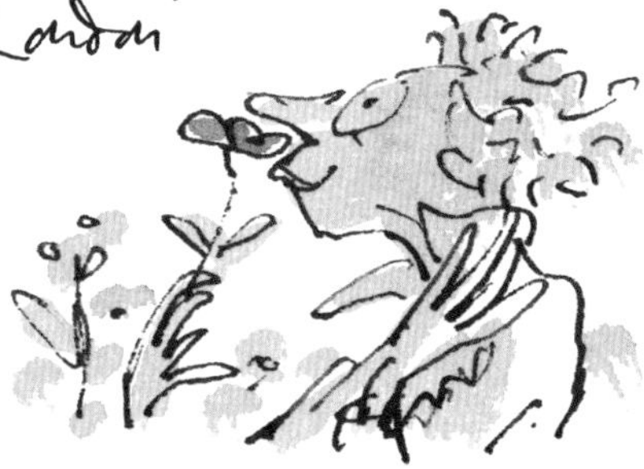

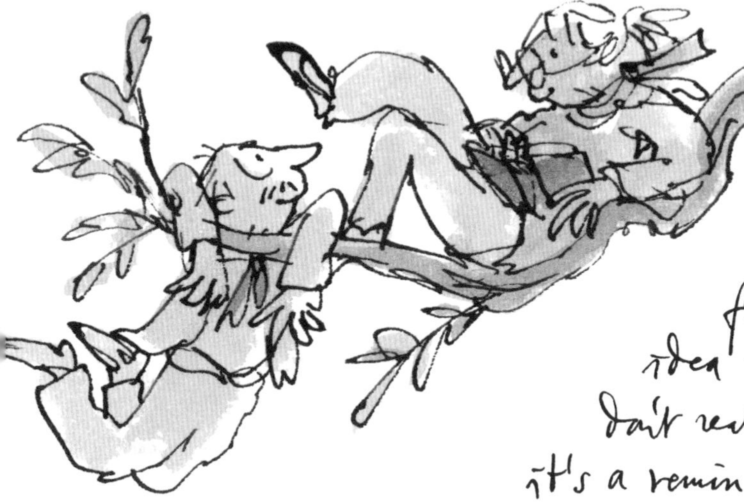

originally from a drawing that I had done for some verses by my friend John Yeoman. I like the idea because, although people of my age don't really spend so much time in trees, it's a reminder that this is not real life but just a visual suggestion — a little metaphor — of the vivacity and élan that can survive even if your limbs don't work with the smoothness & efficiency that they used to. (I am not, of course, trying to pretend that age is this amount of fun all the time.)

I owe heartfelt thanks to Stephen Barnham and to Dr Nick Rhodes of the Nightingale Project who introduced me to the possibility of illustrating the walls of hospitals; to Christine Baker who immediately saw these pictures as a book; and to Klaus Flugge of the Andersen Press whose spontaneous enthusiasm and understanding set me swinging from branch to branch. Metaphorically, of course.

QB : 2008

À la Carte

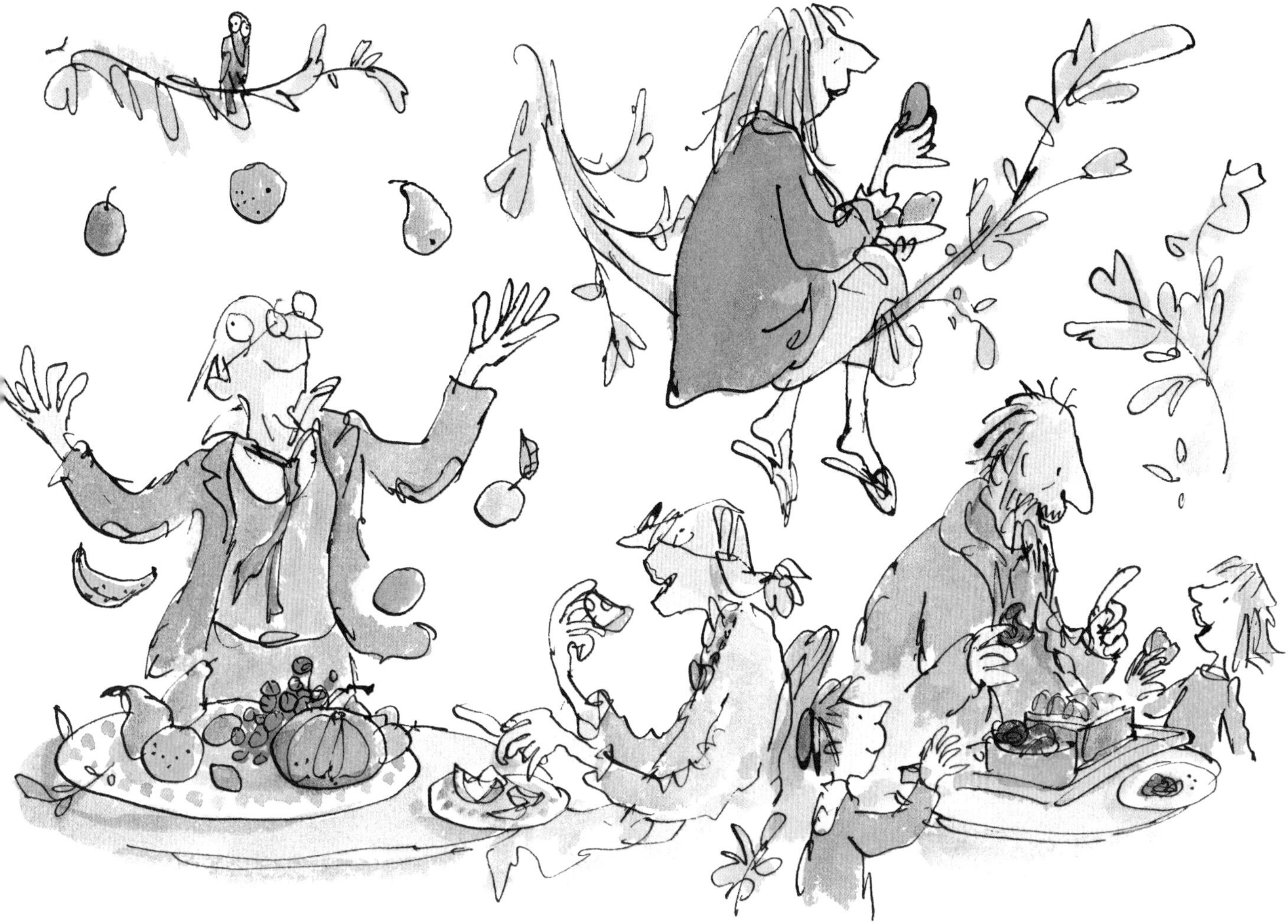

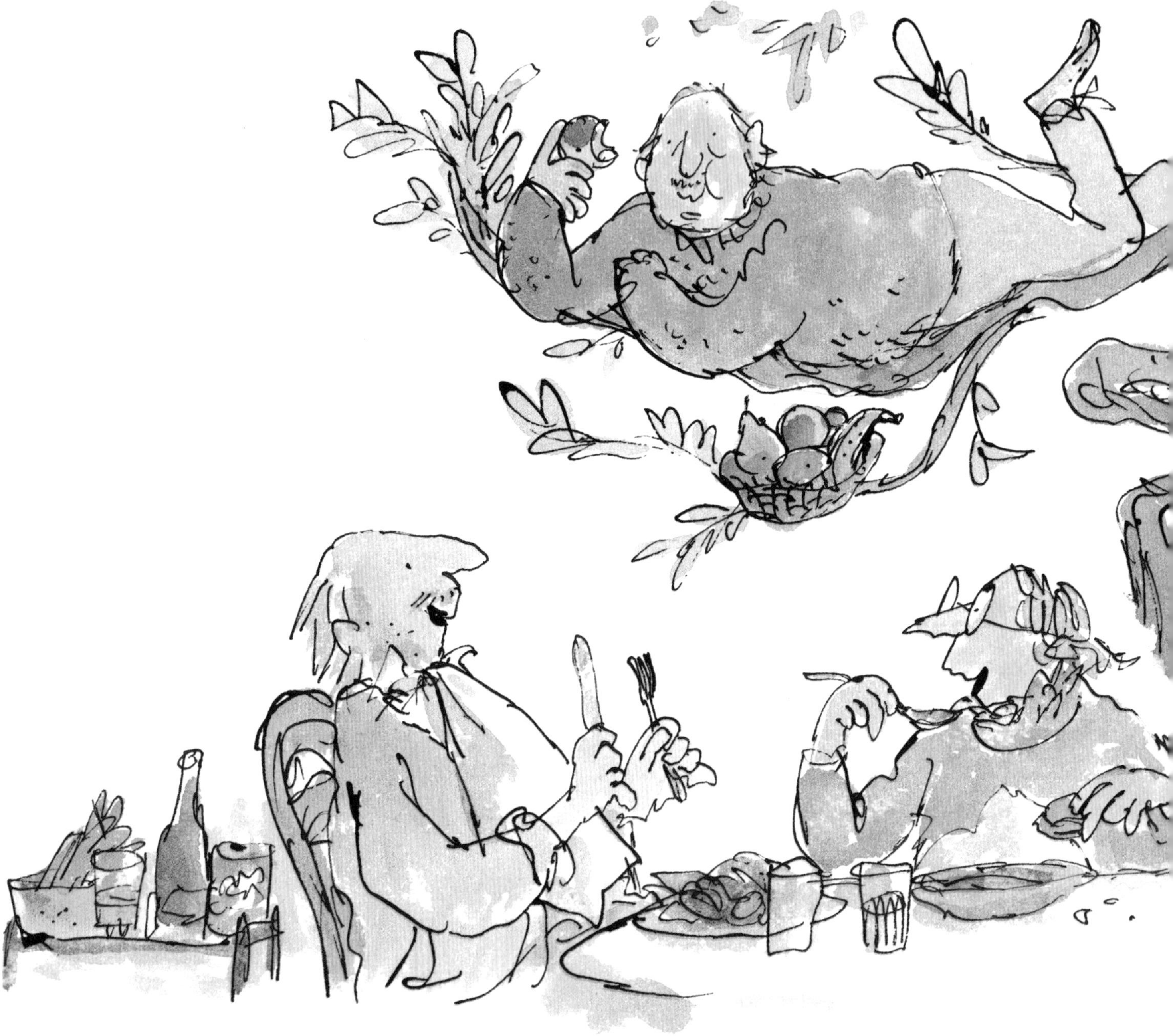

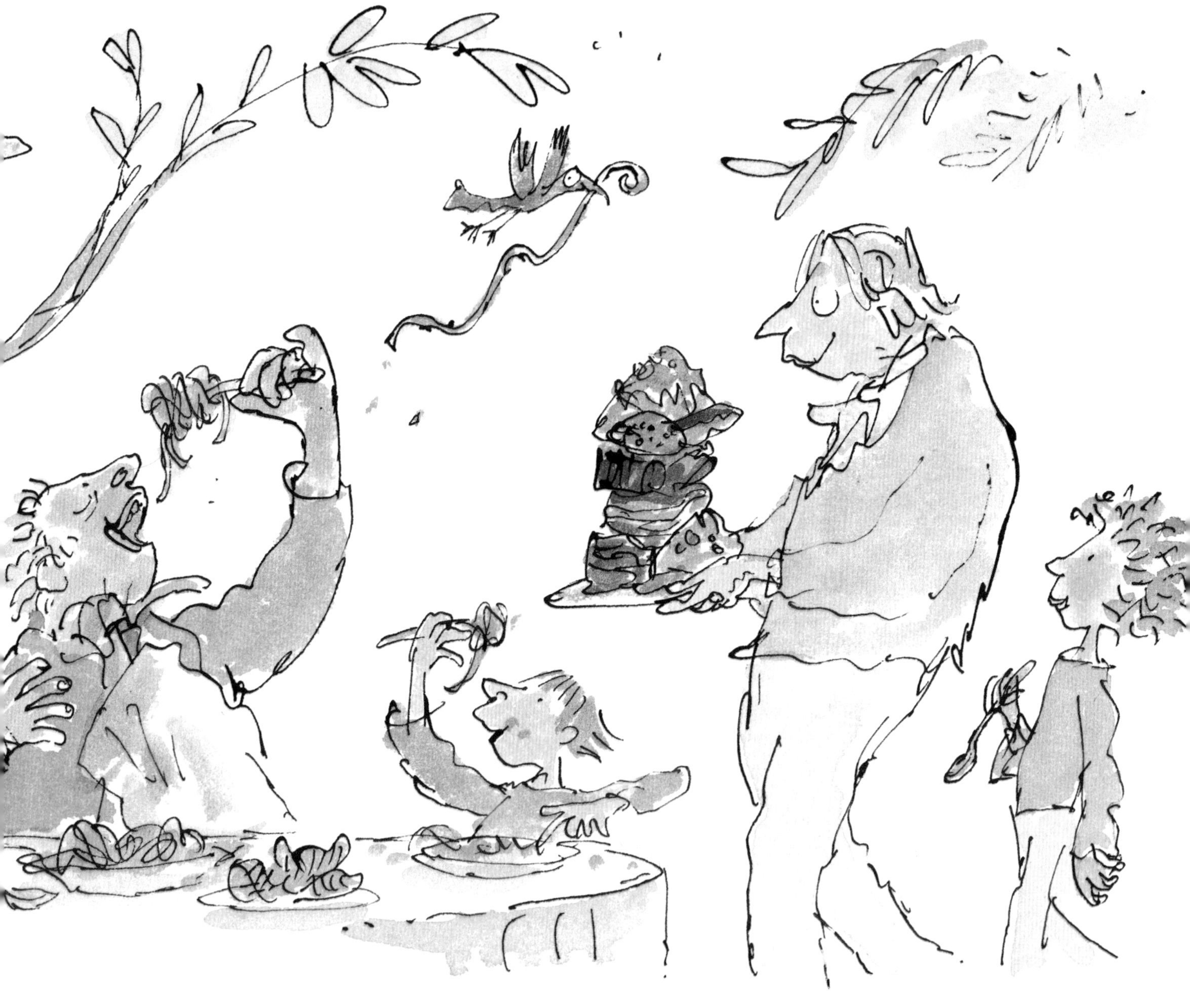

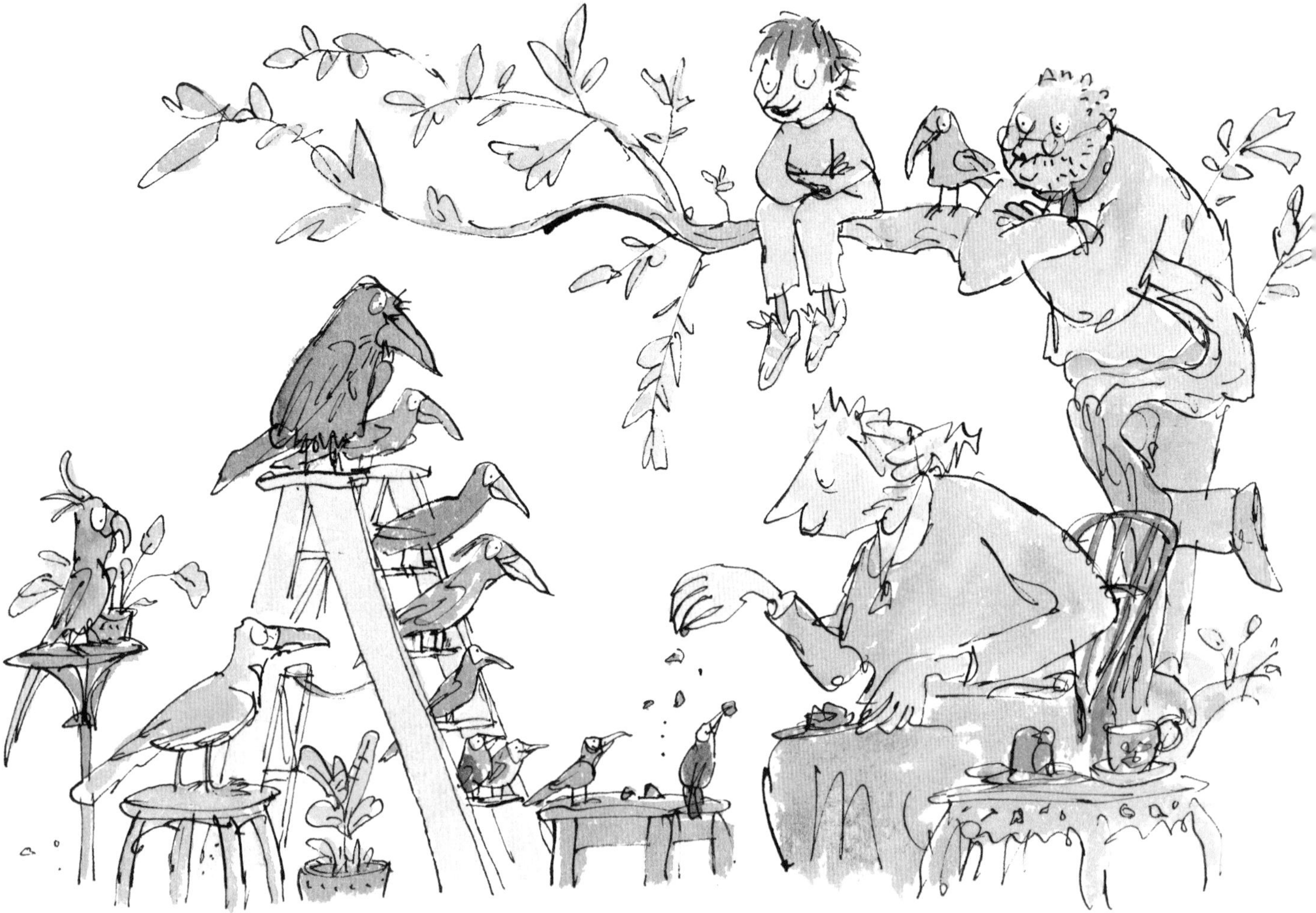

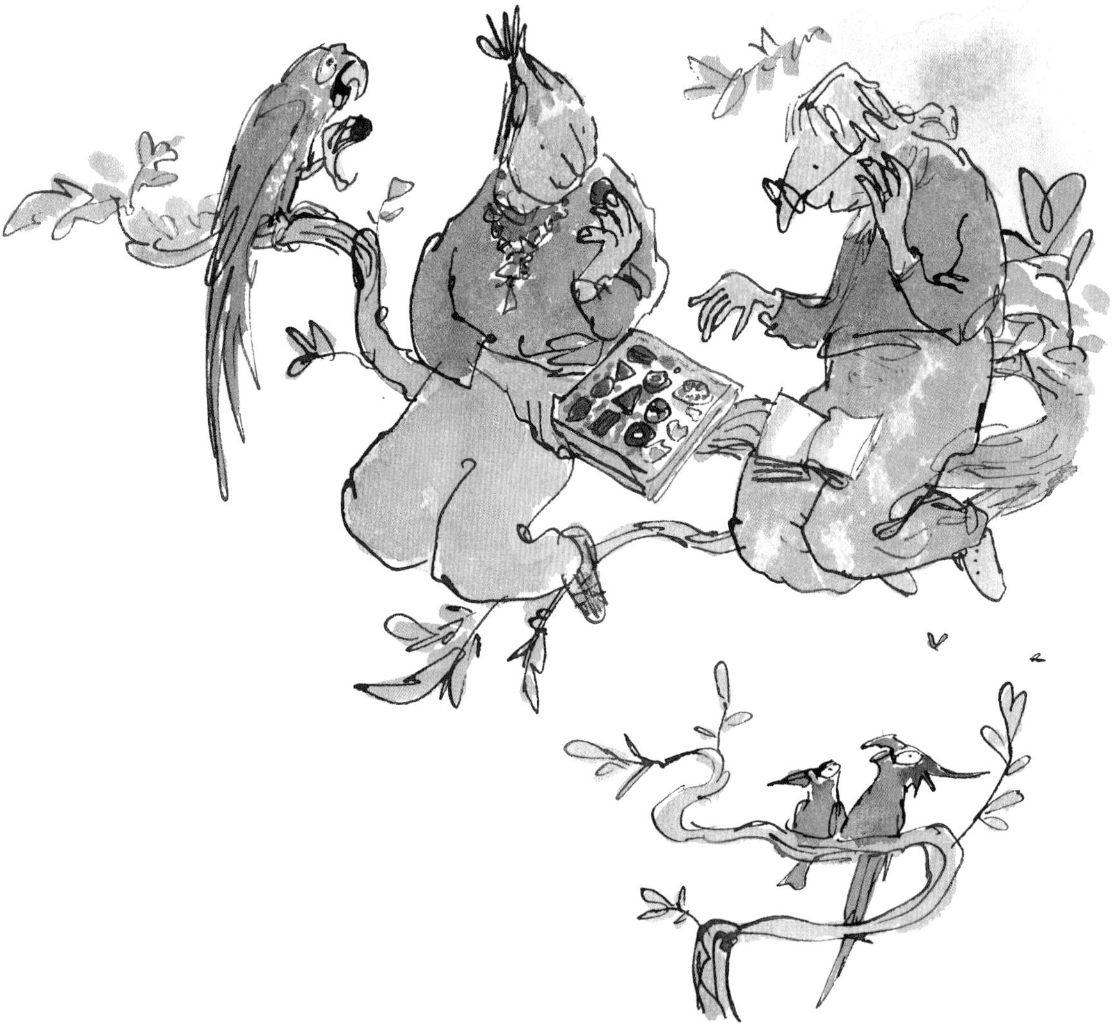

Out of Doors

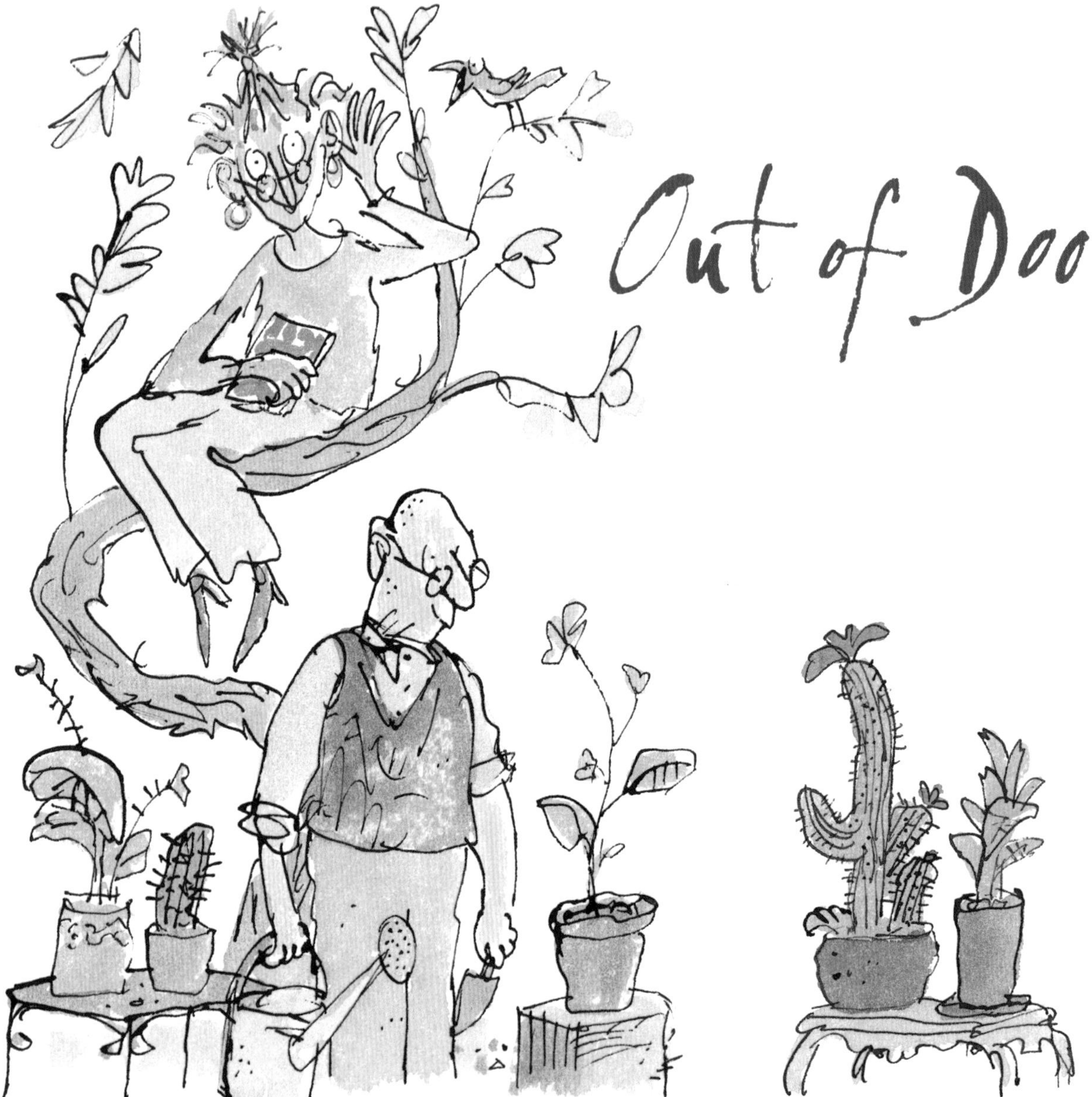

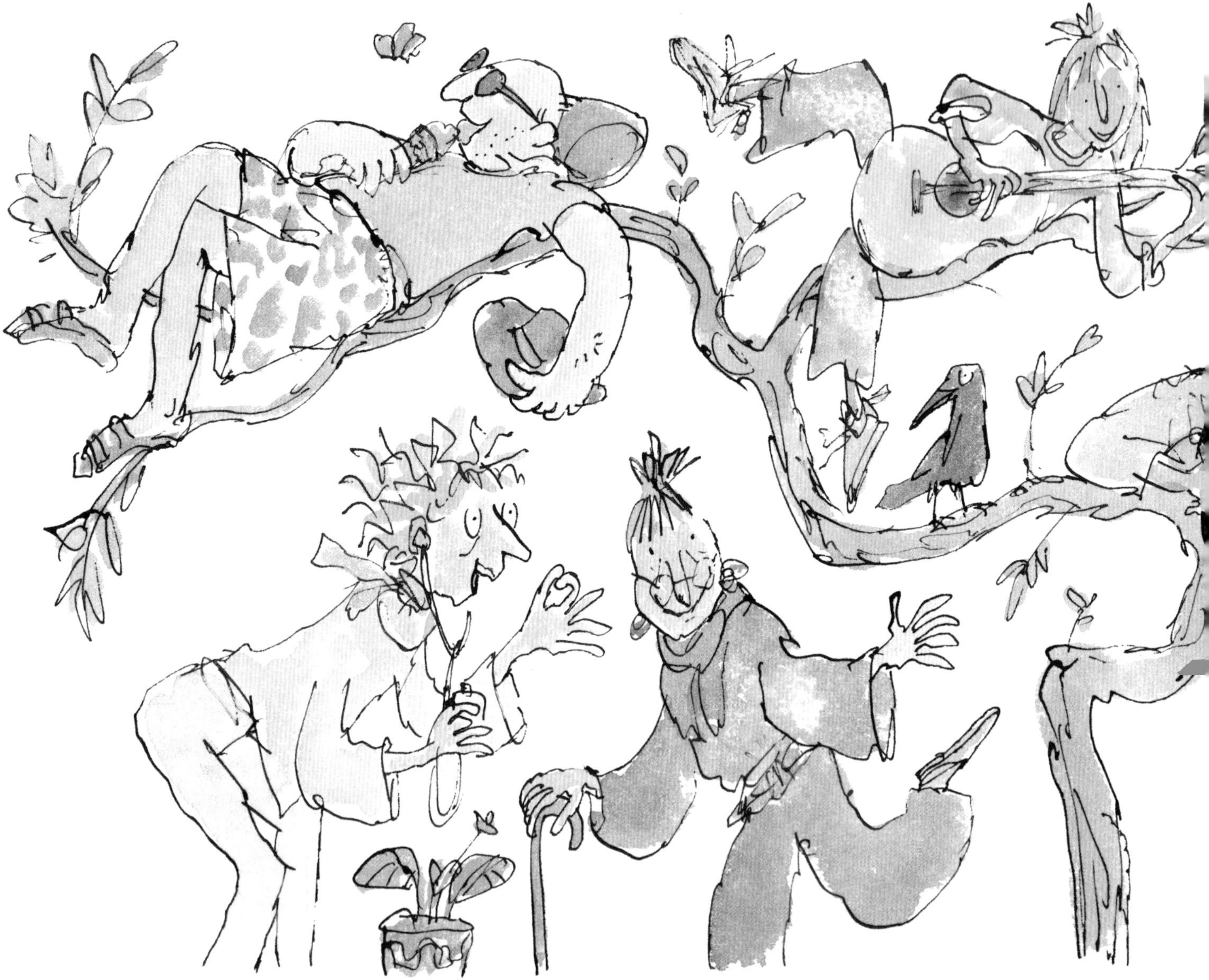

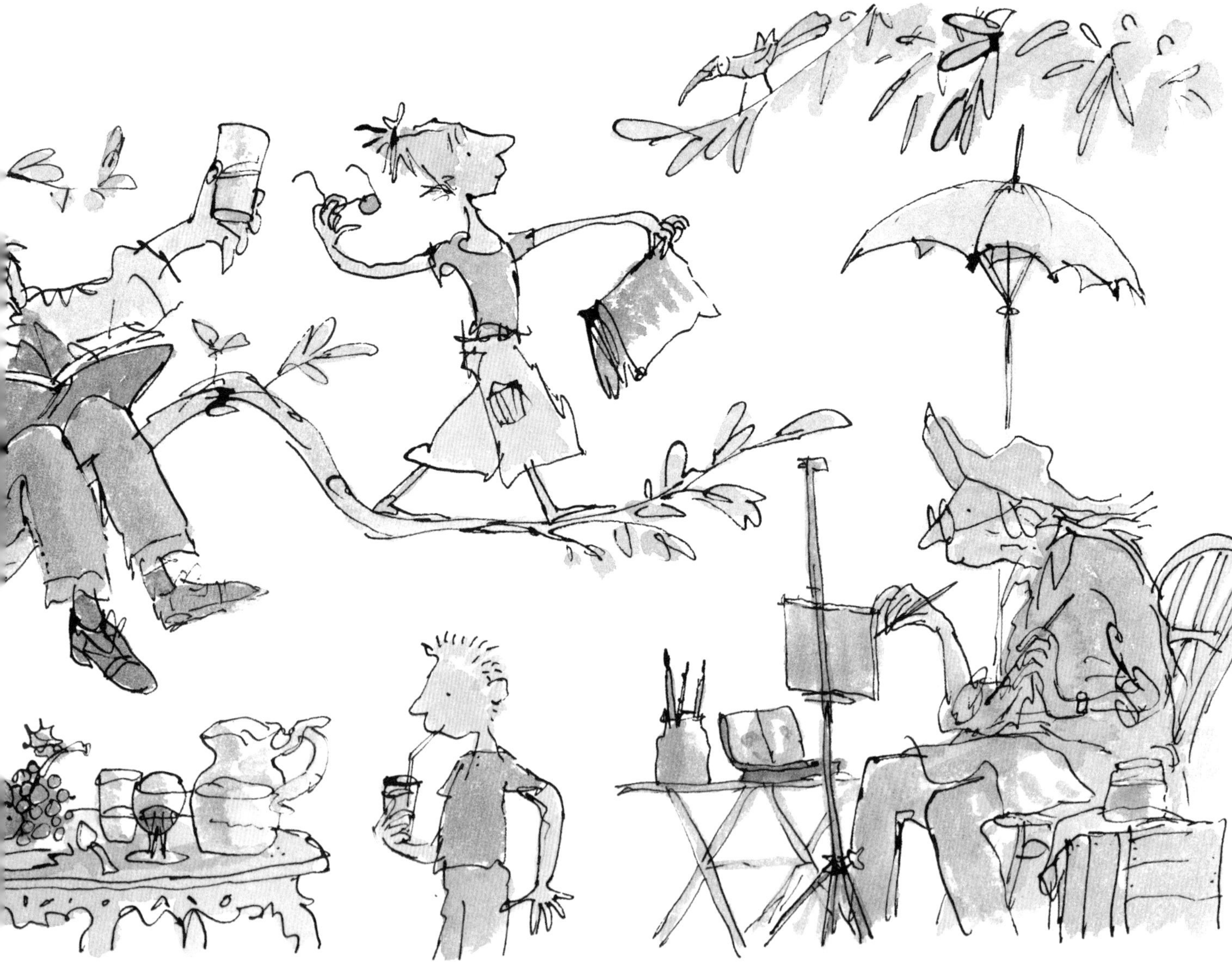

Keeping Fit

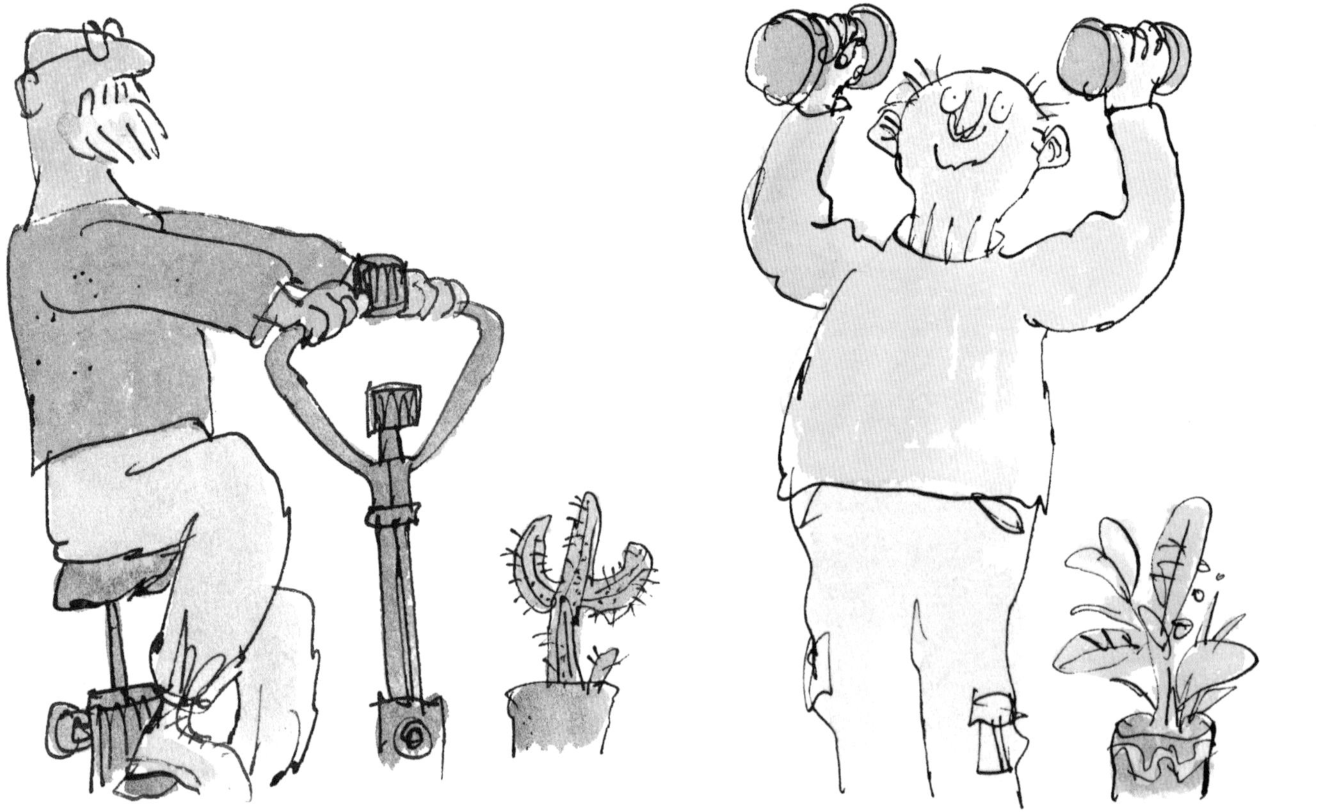

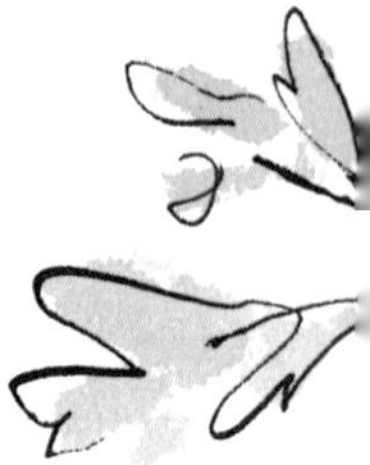

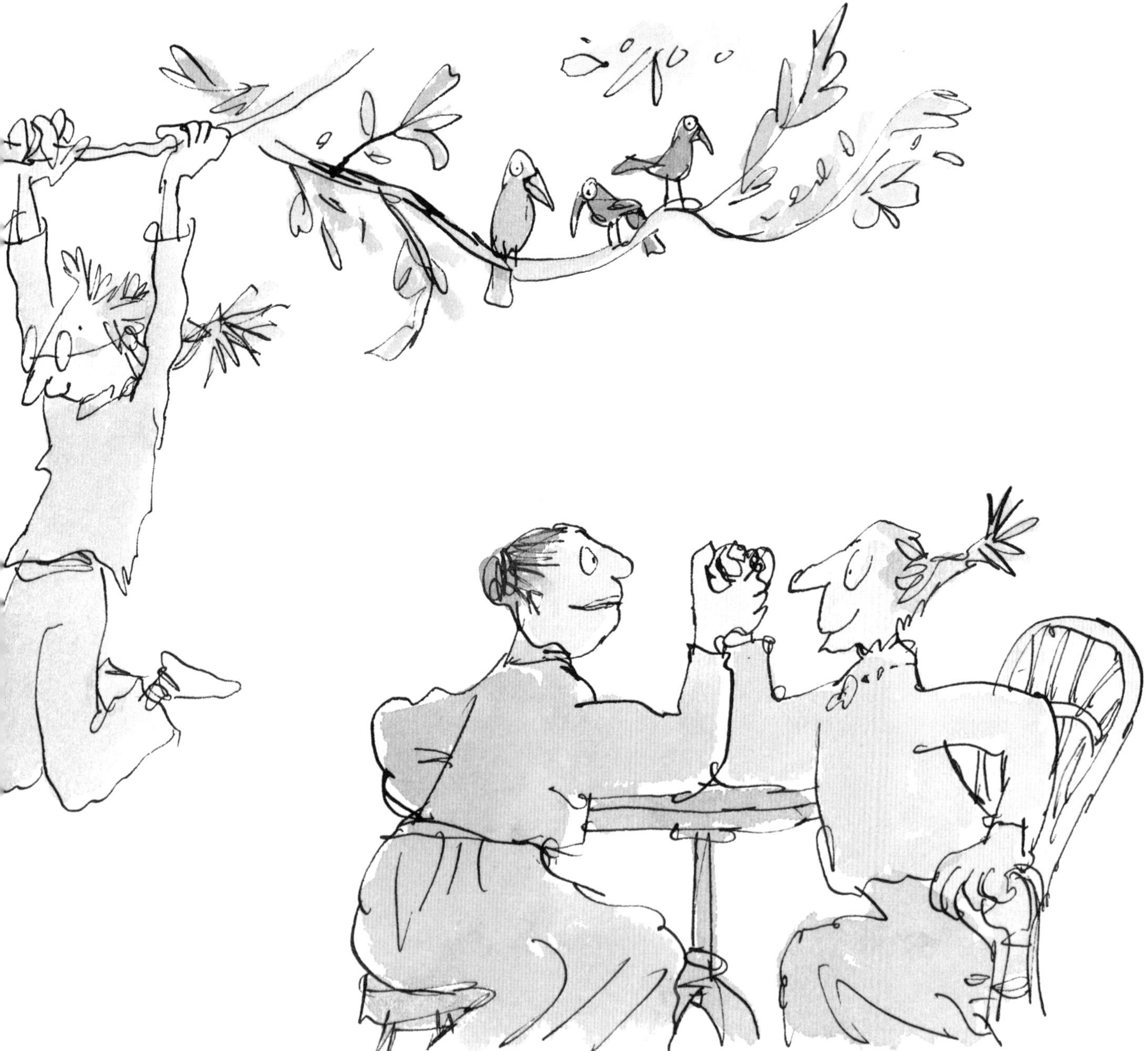

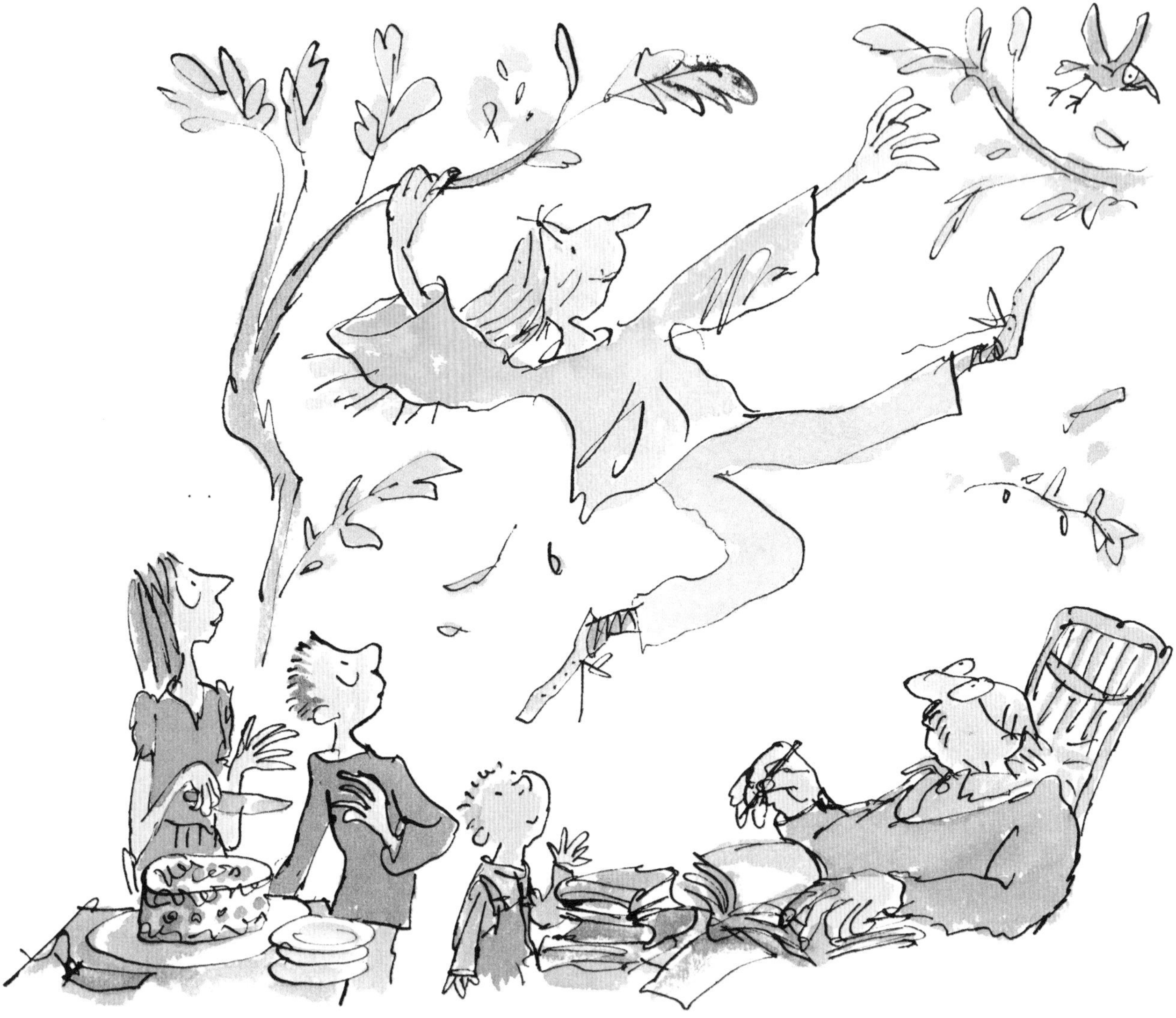

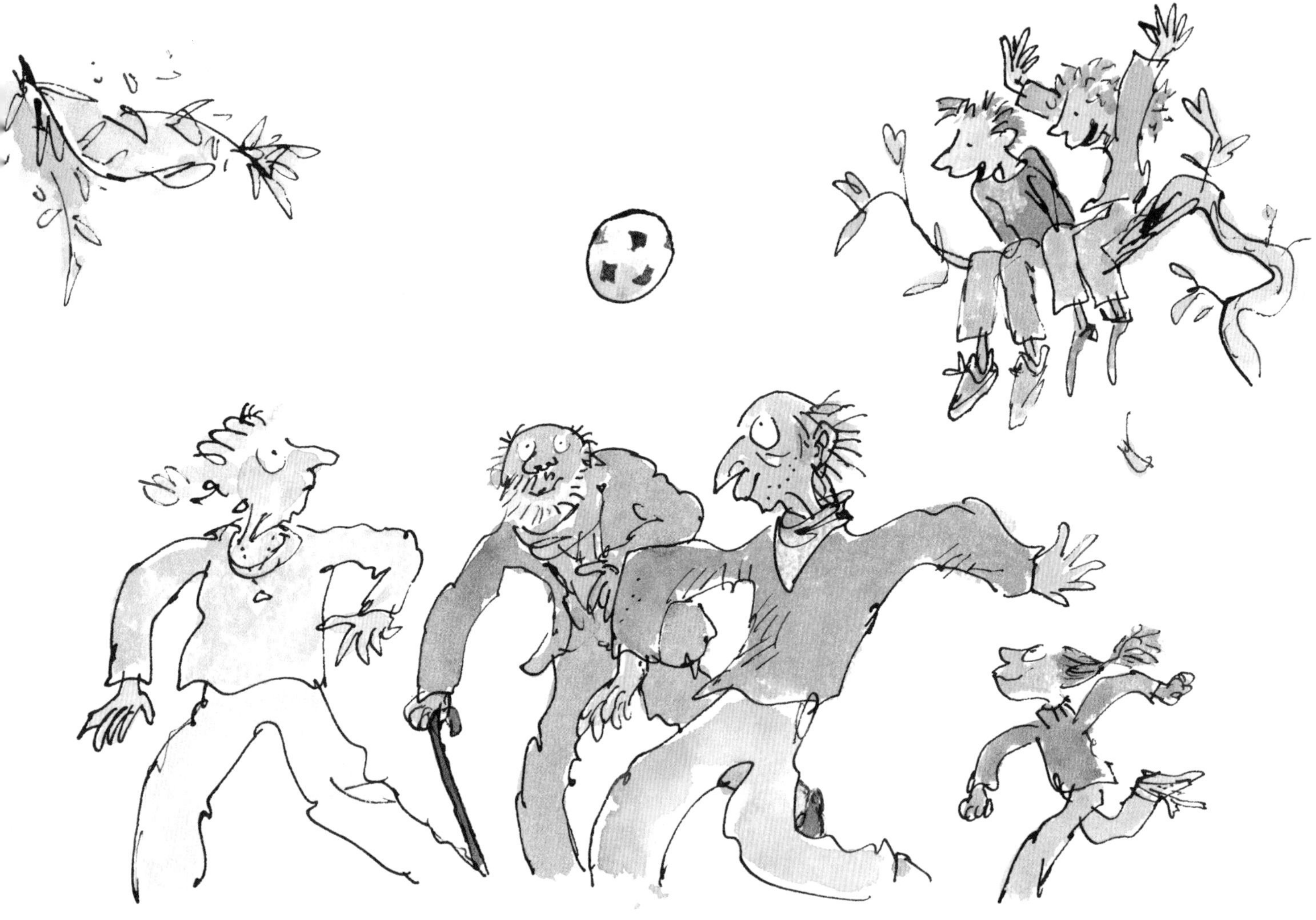

Tell Me a Story

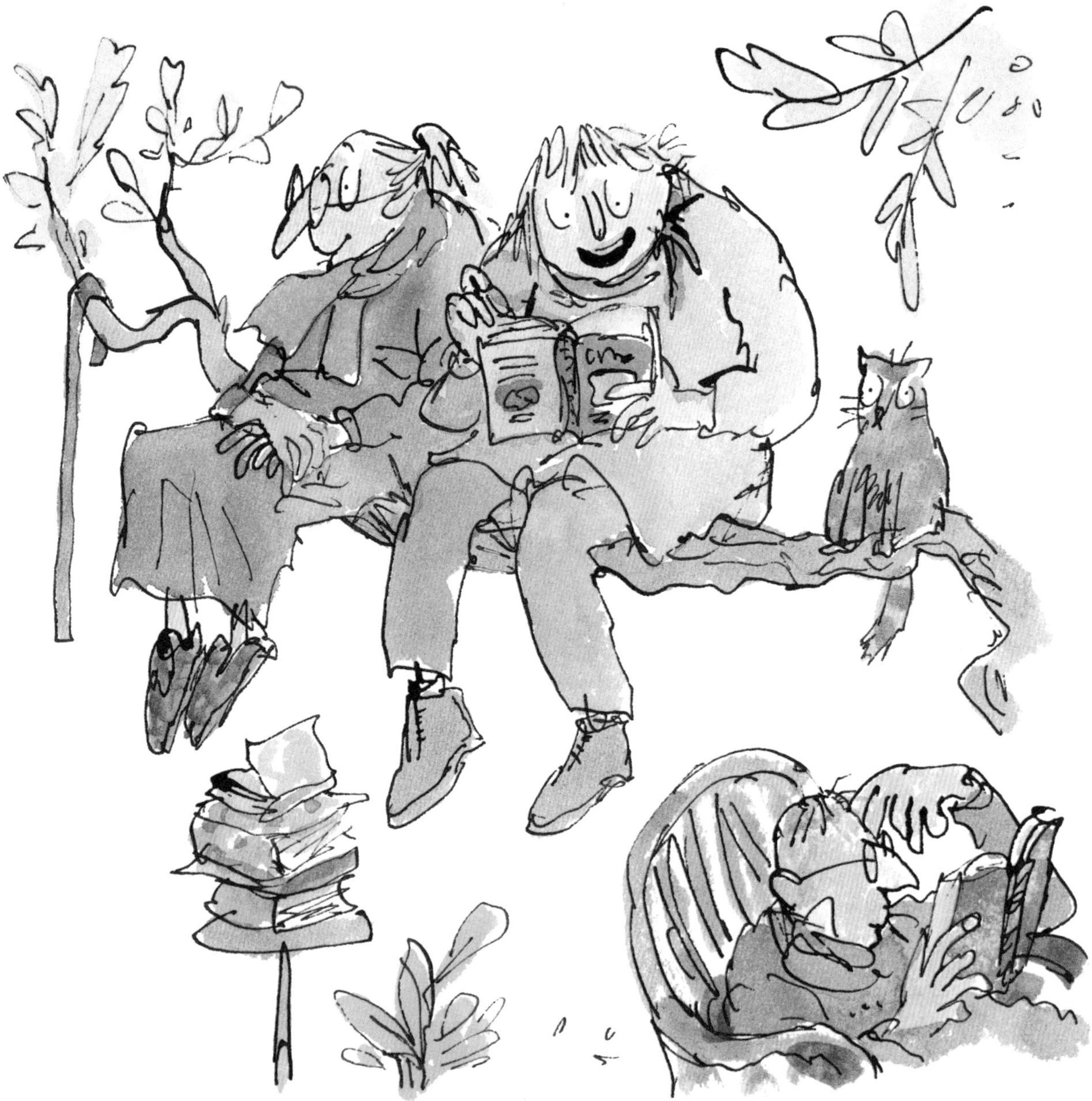

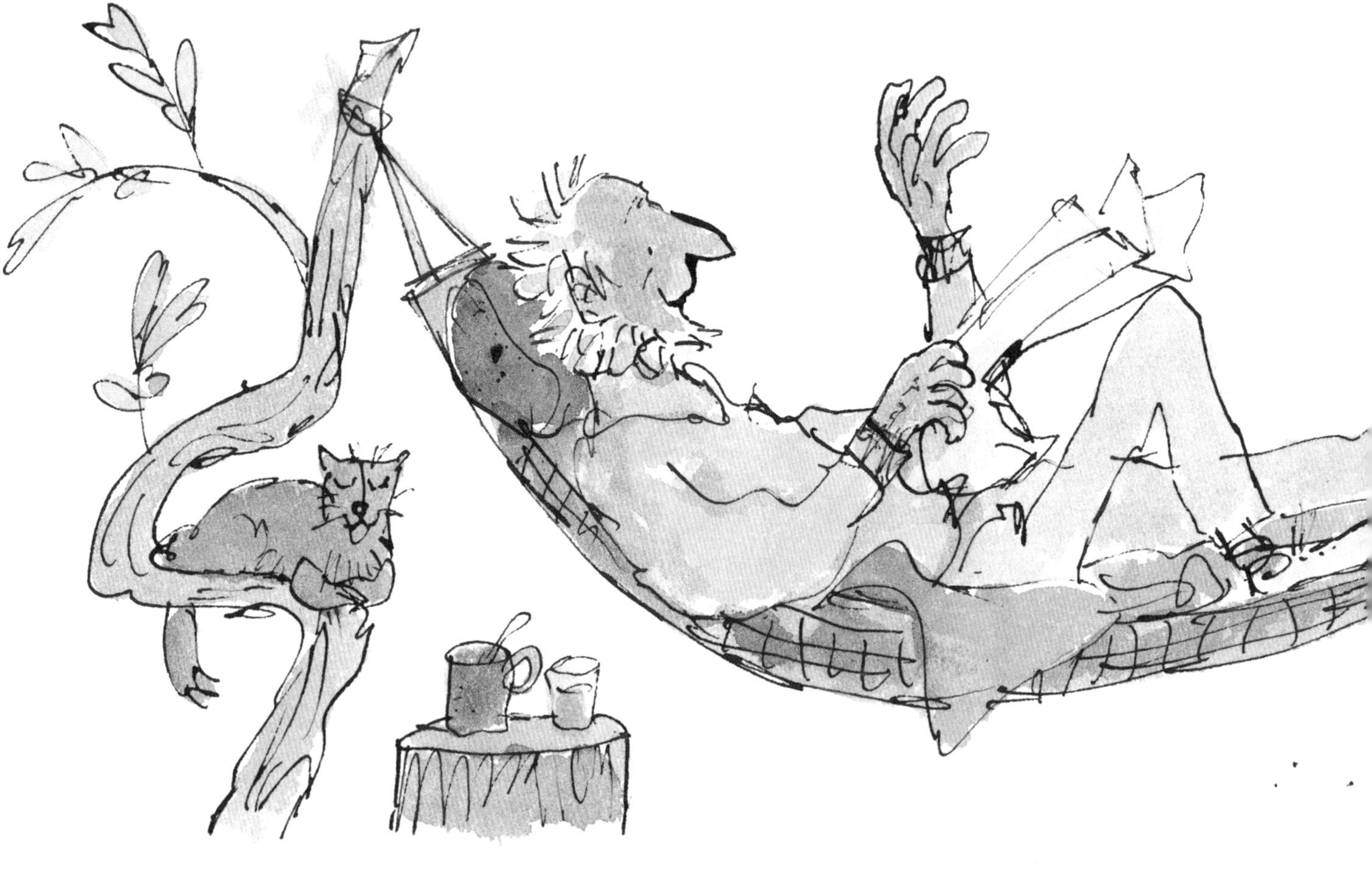

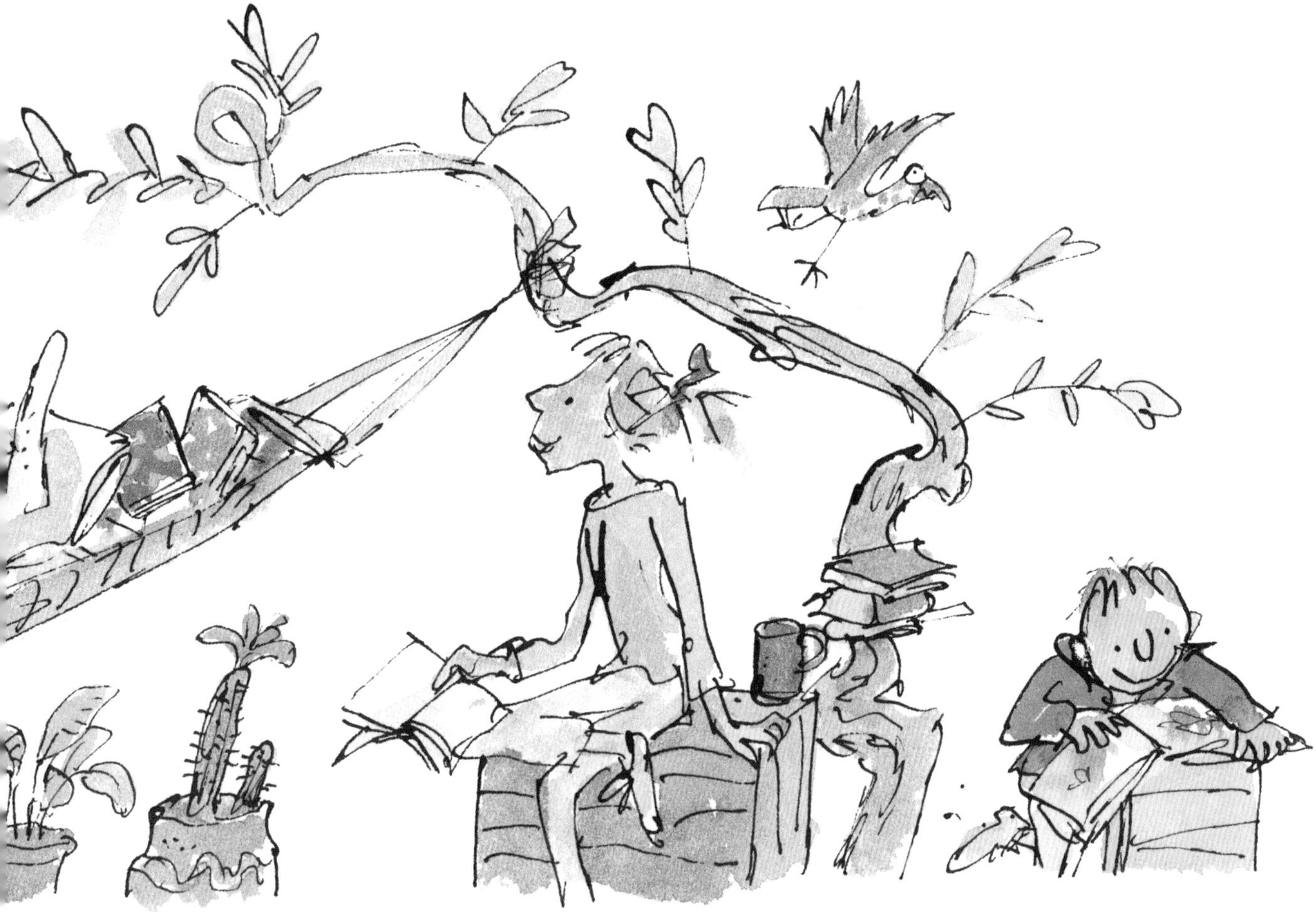

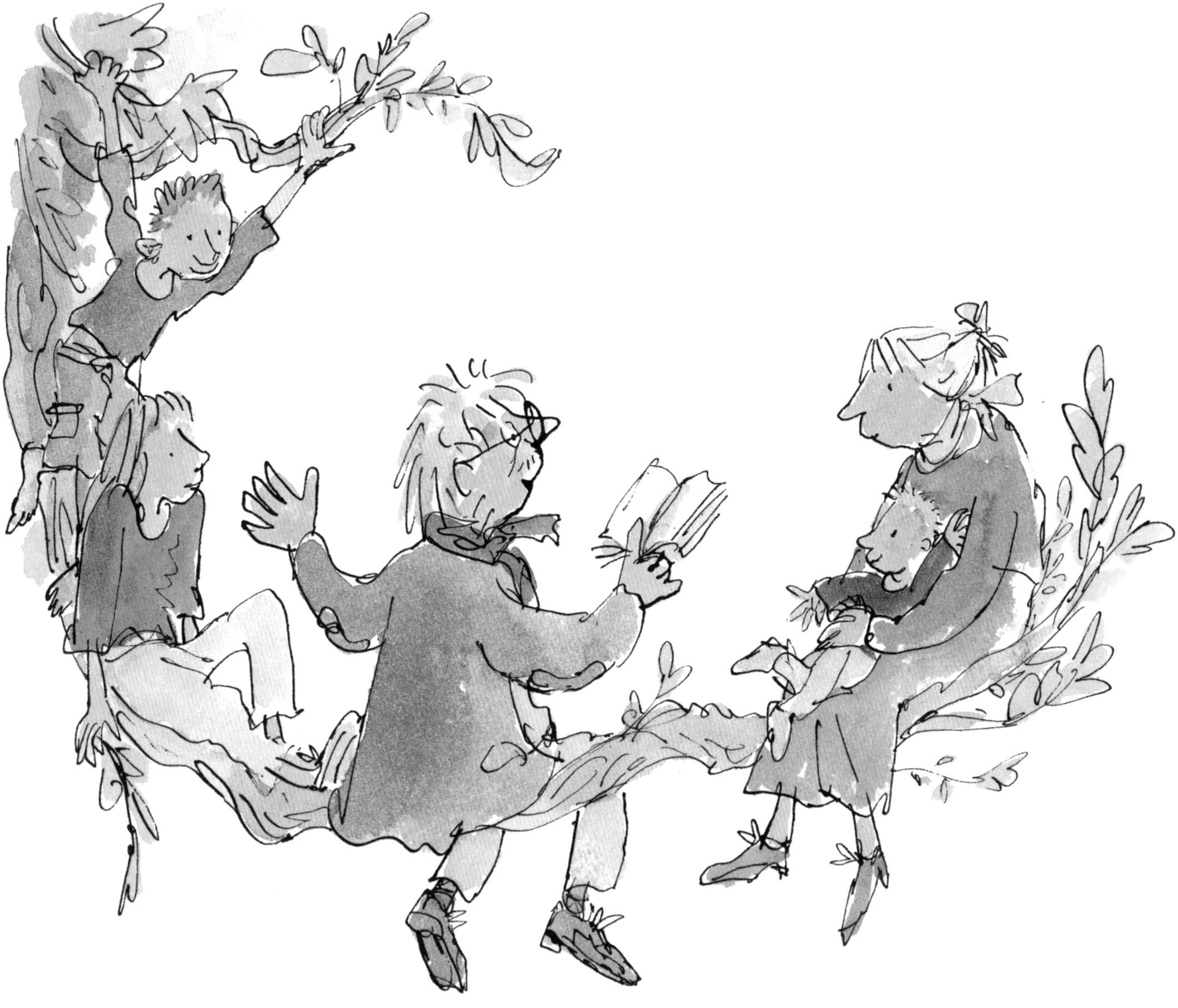

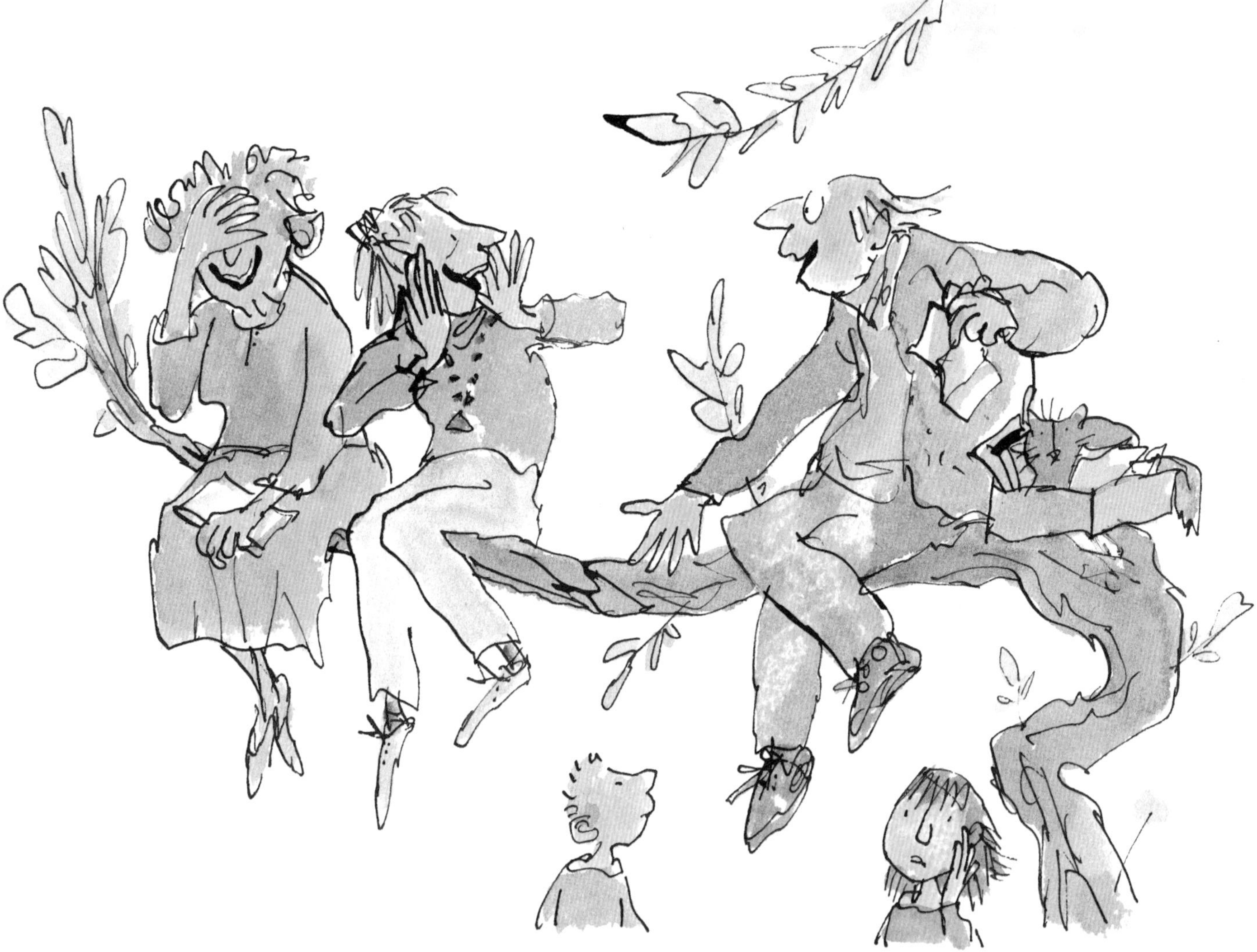

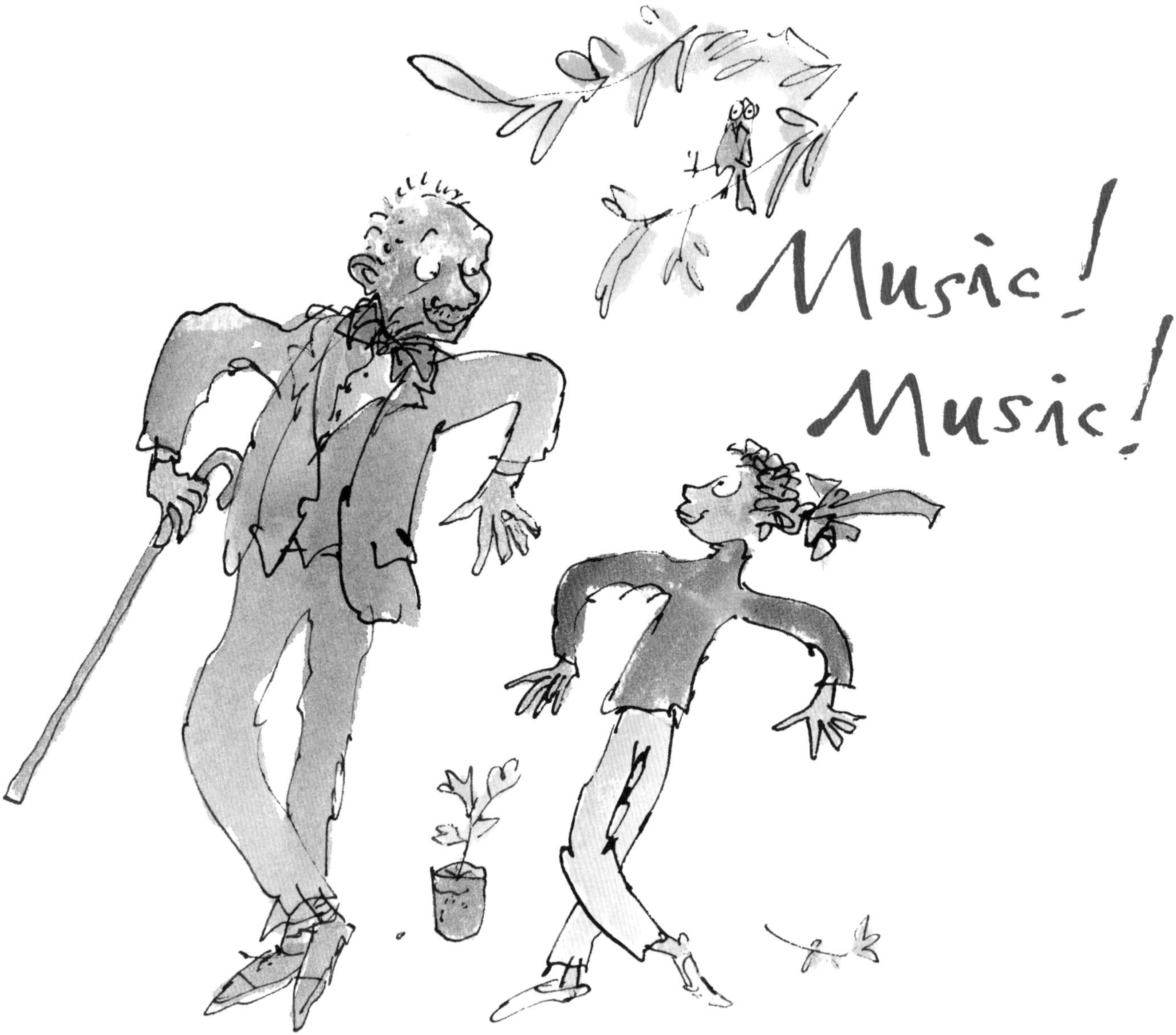
Music!
Music!

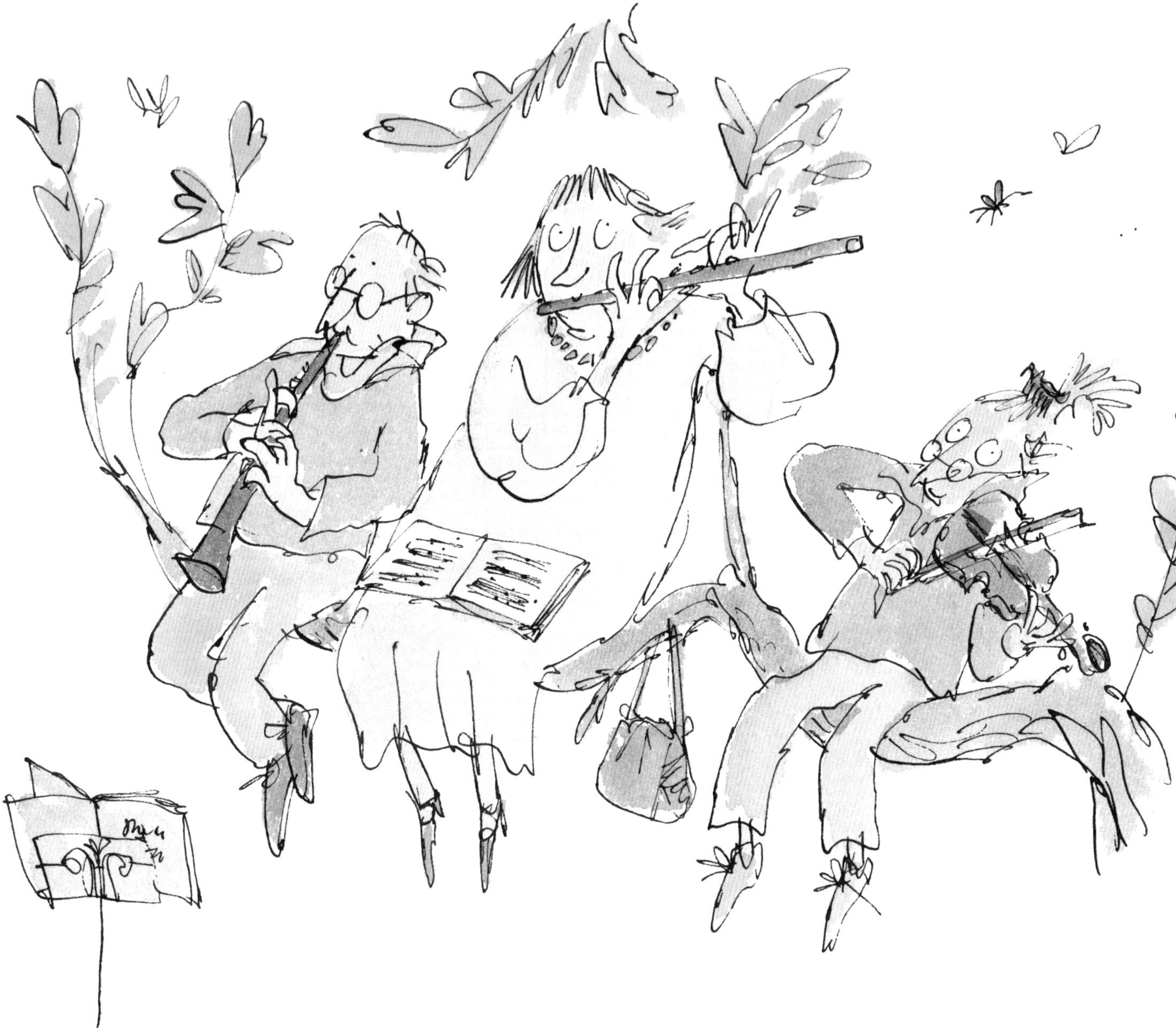

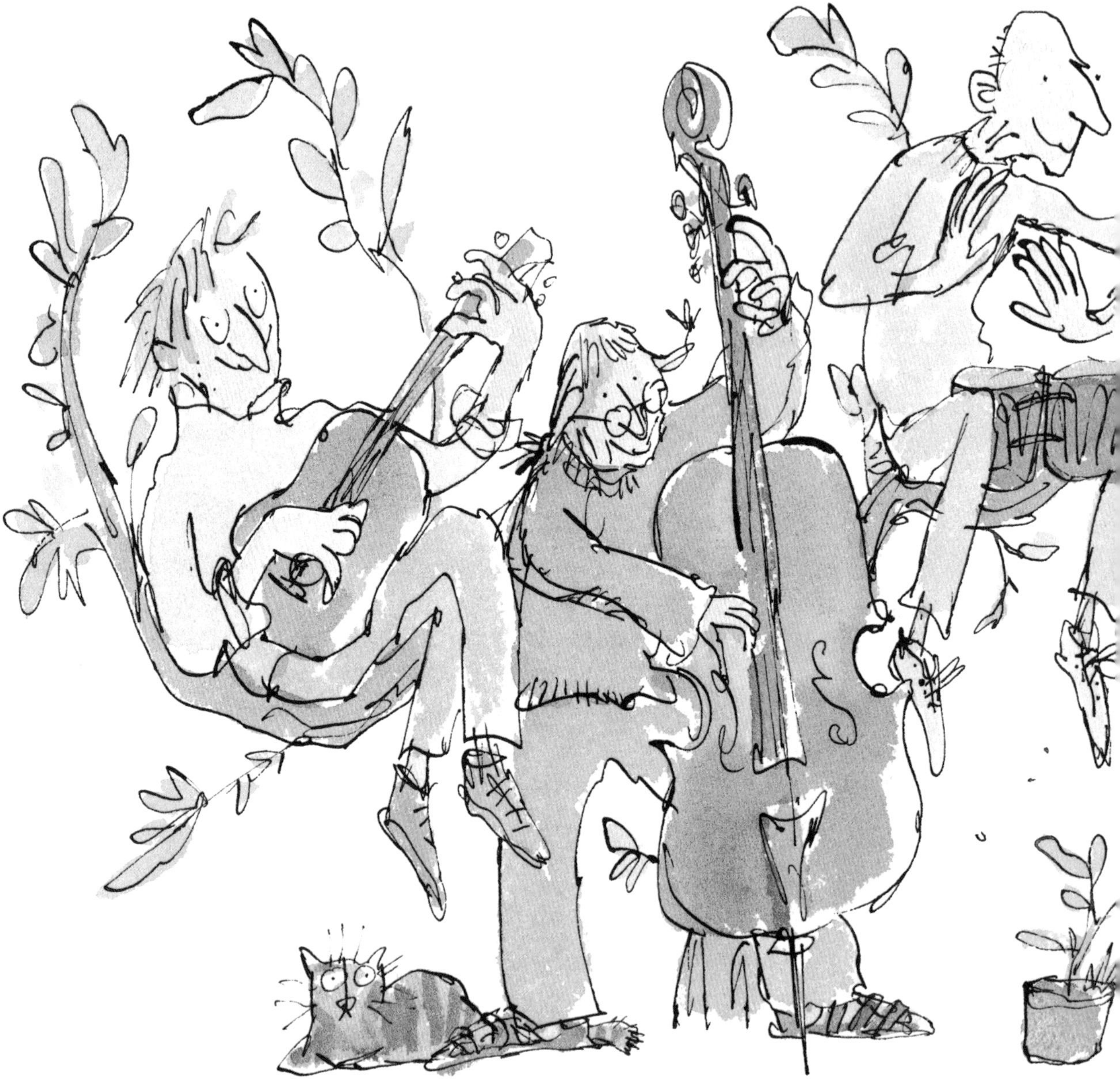

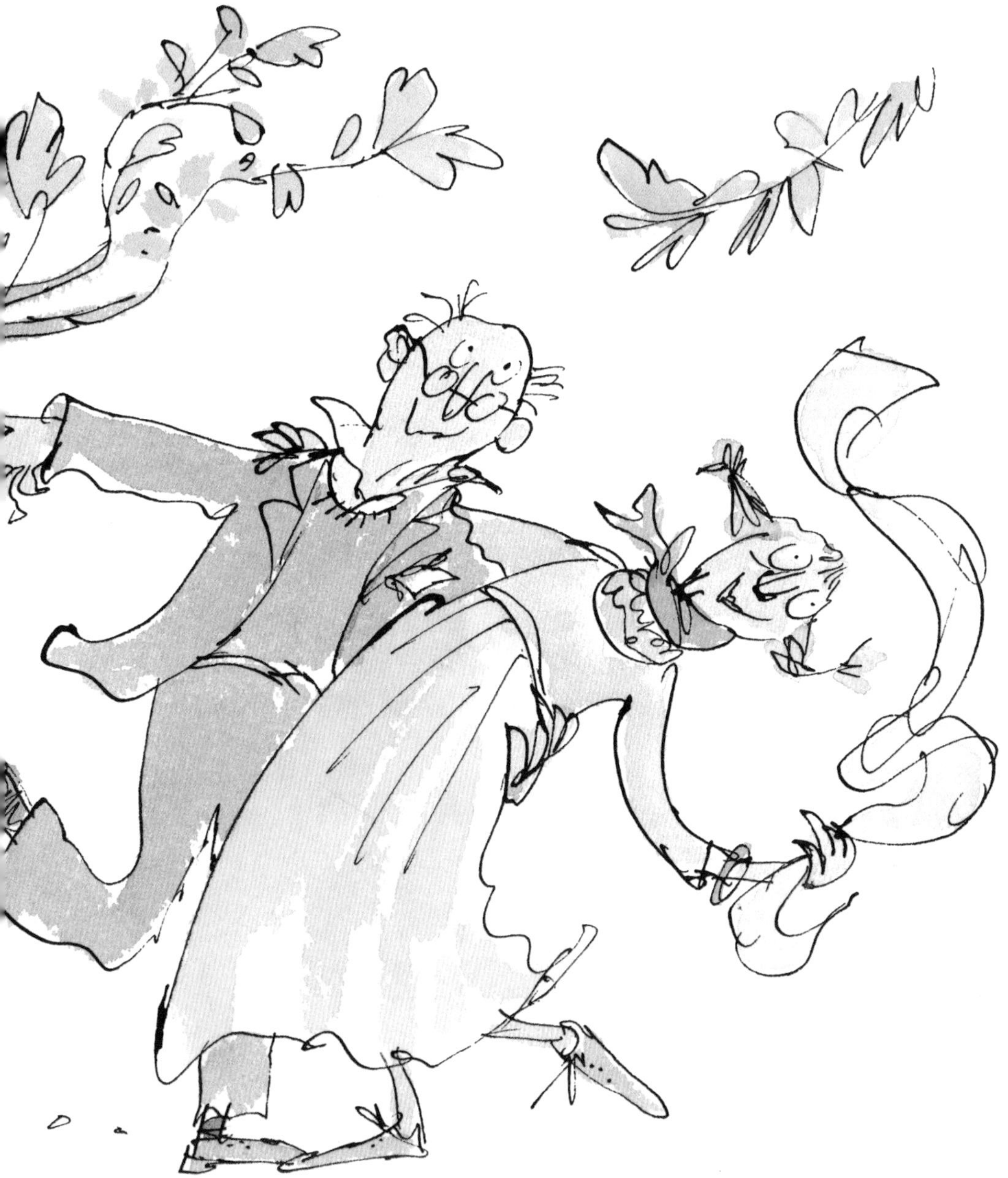

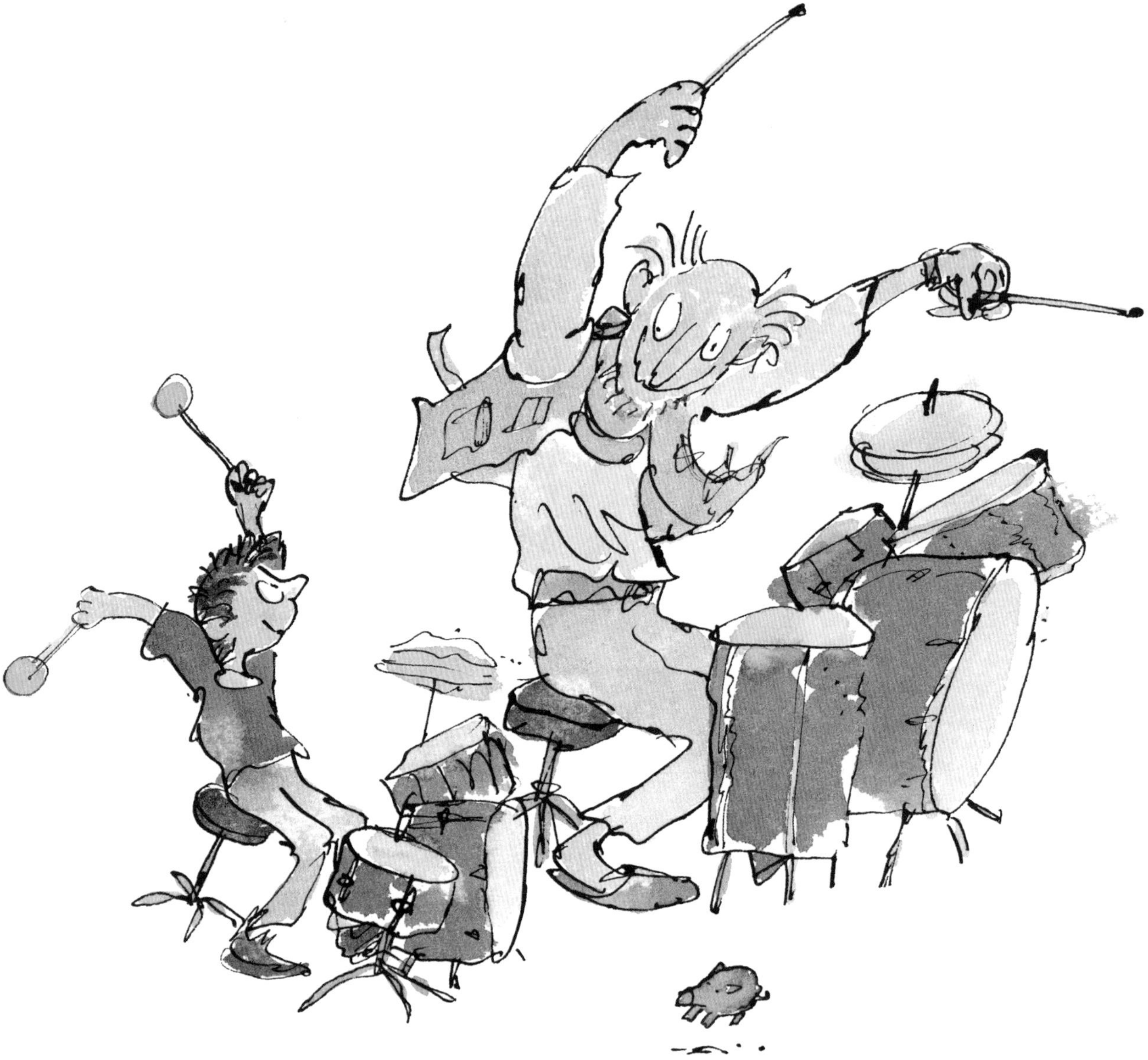

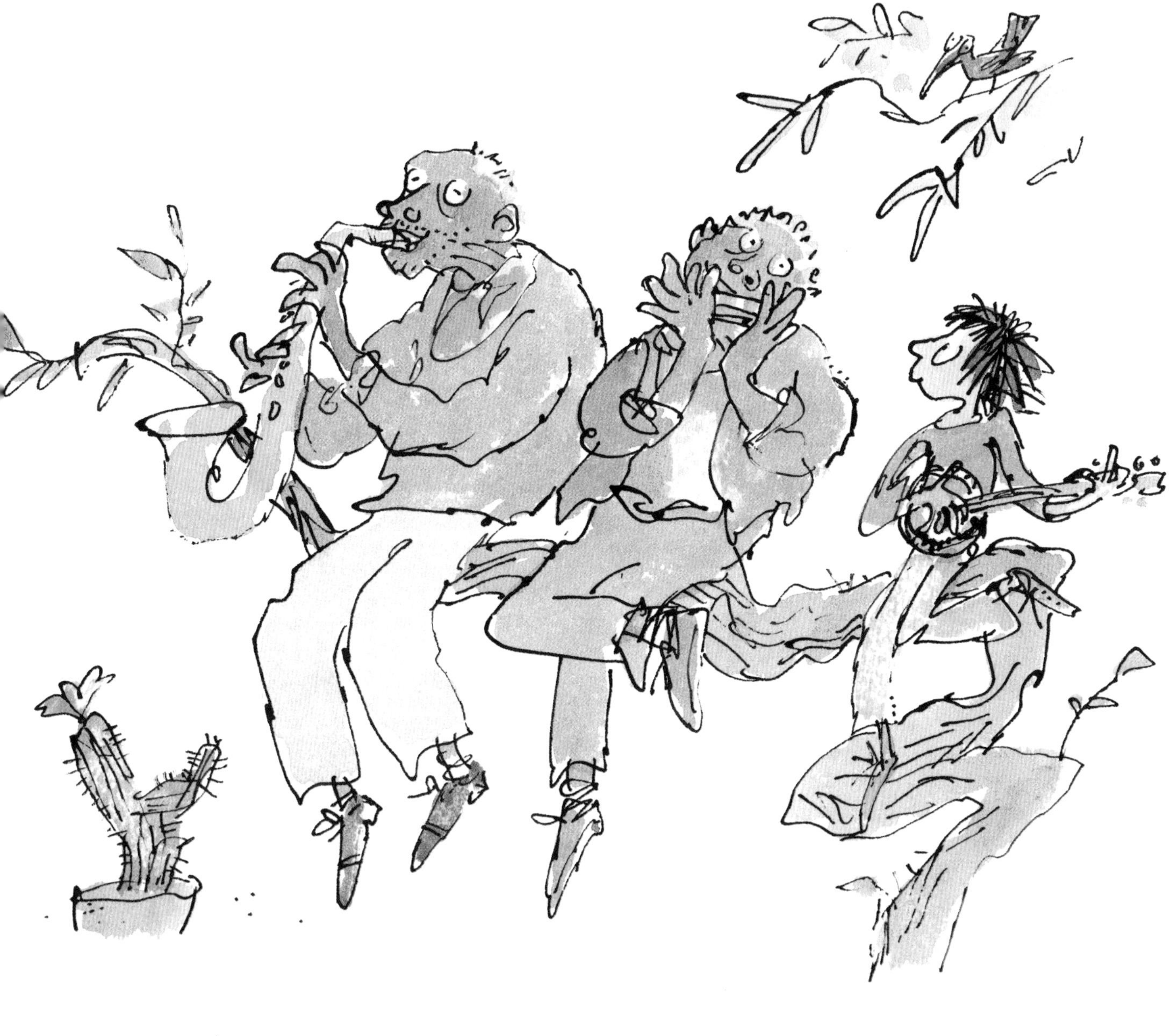

The Art of Self-Expression

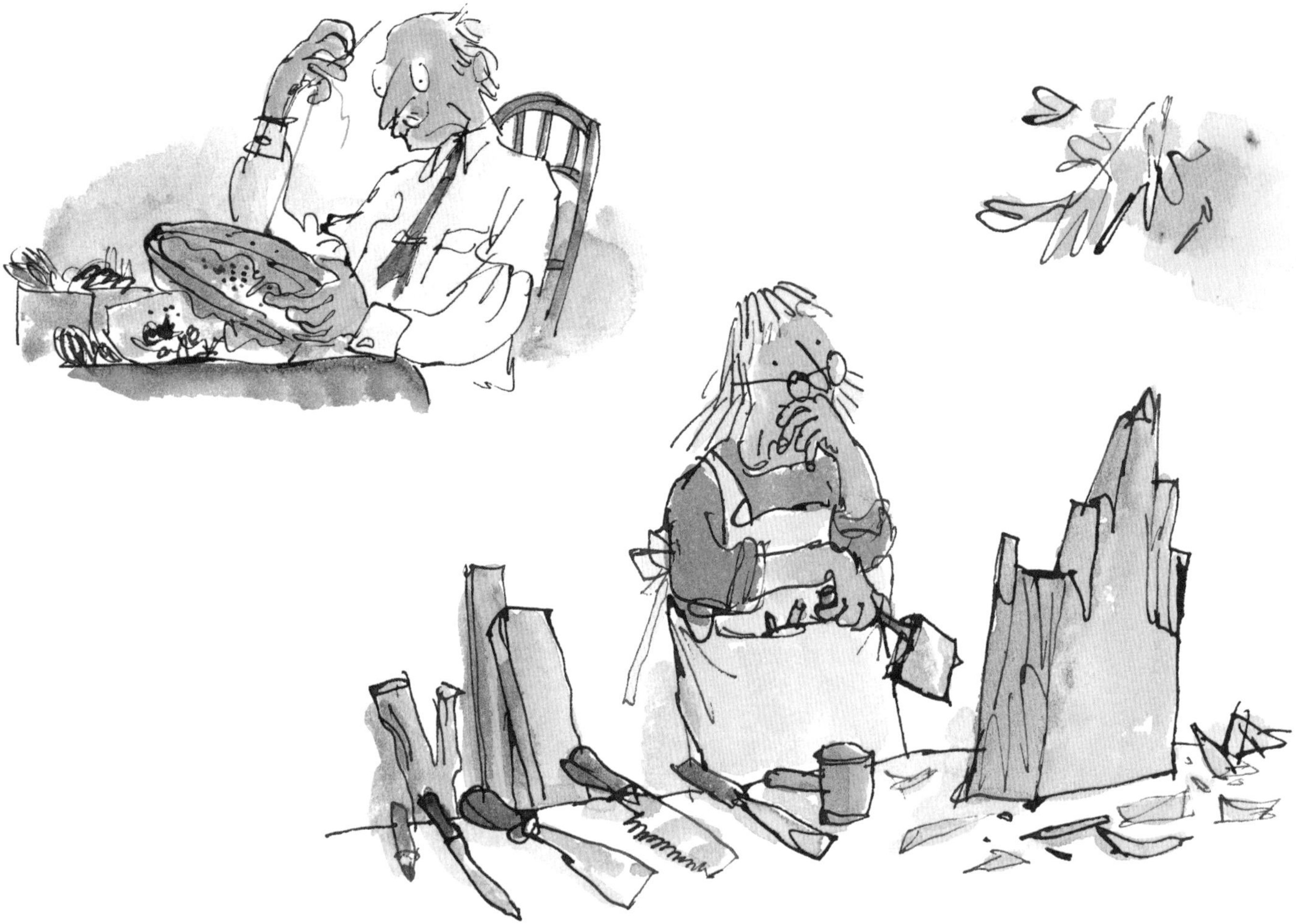

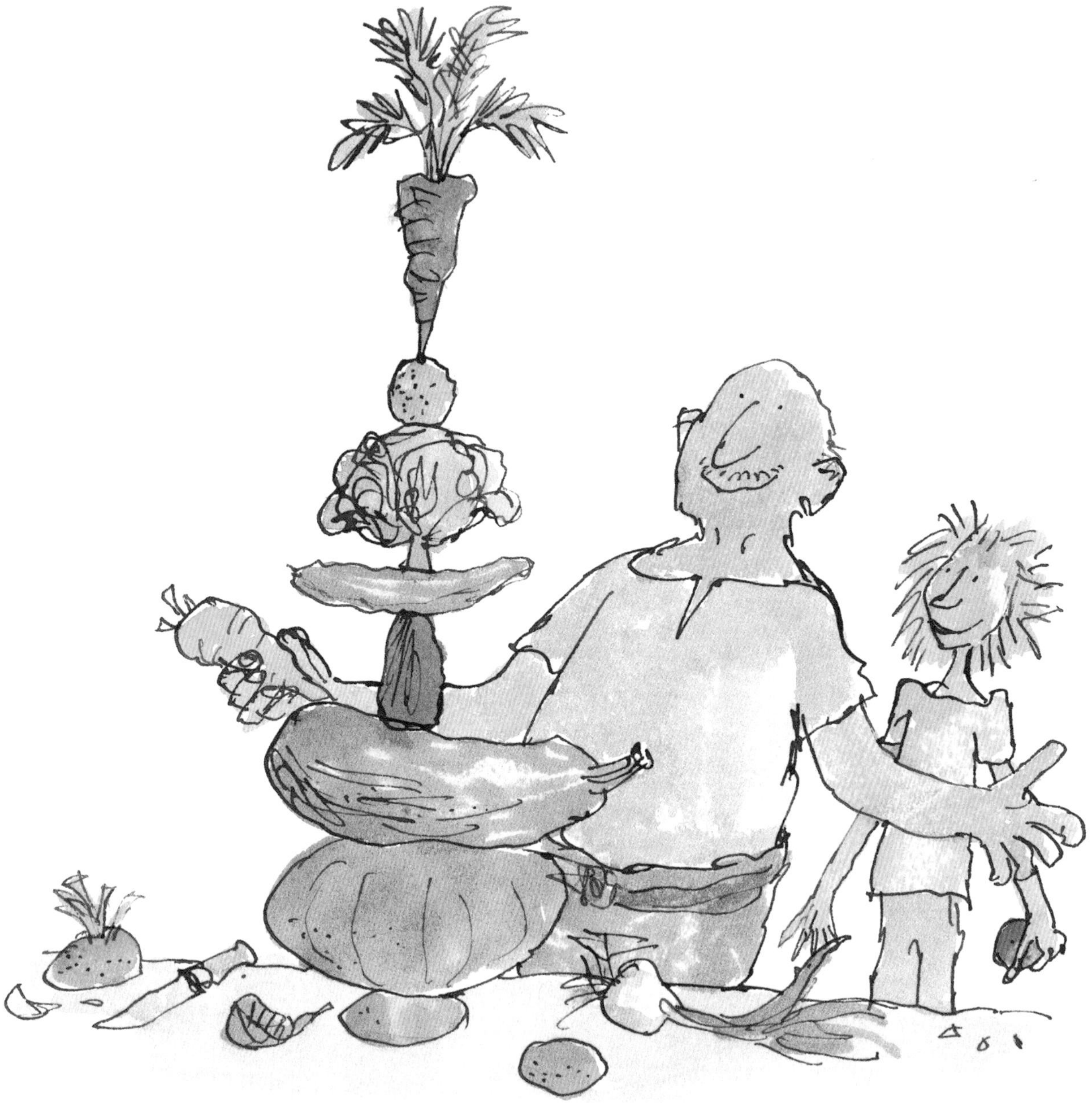

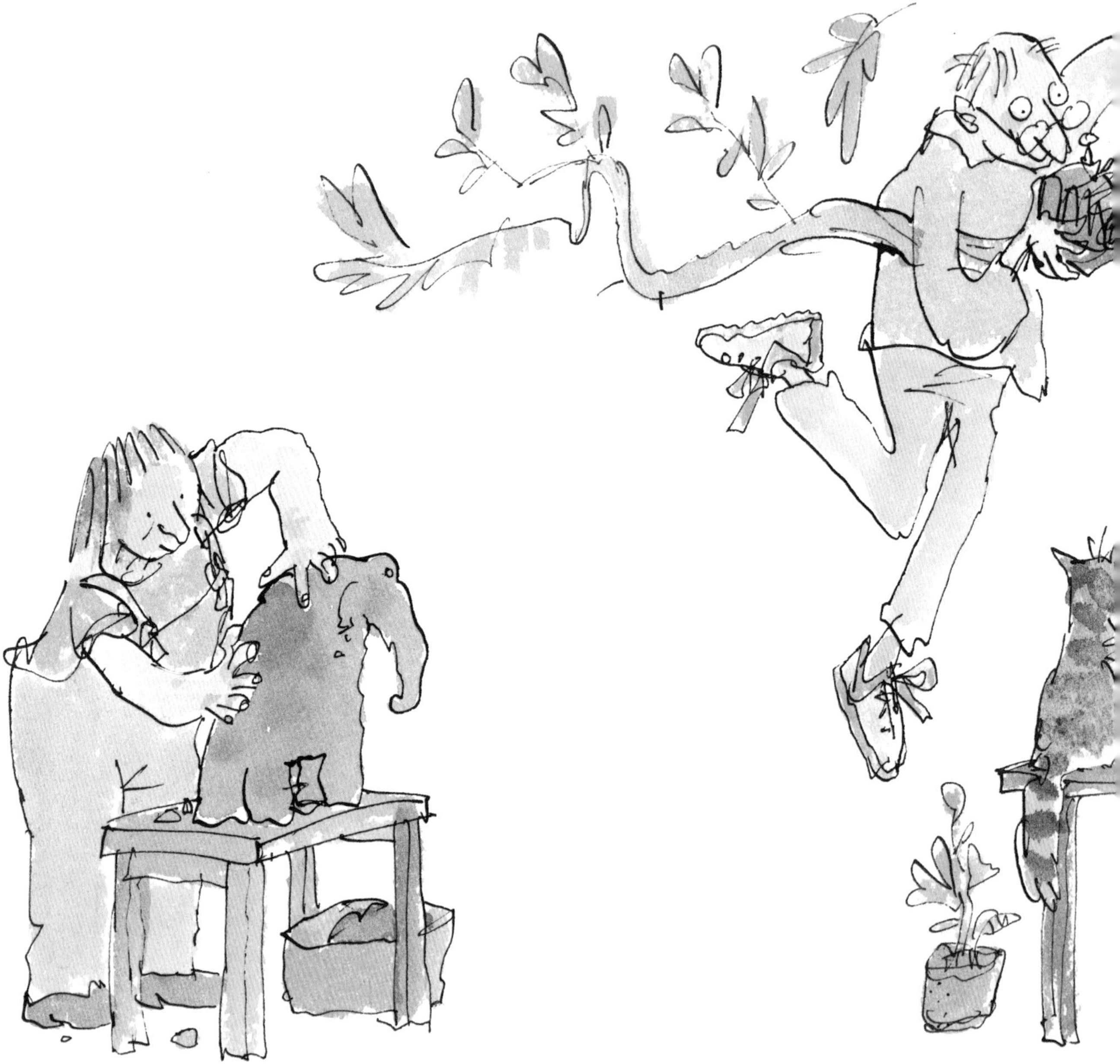

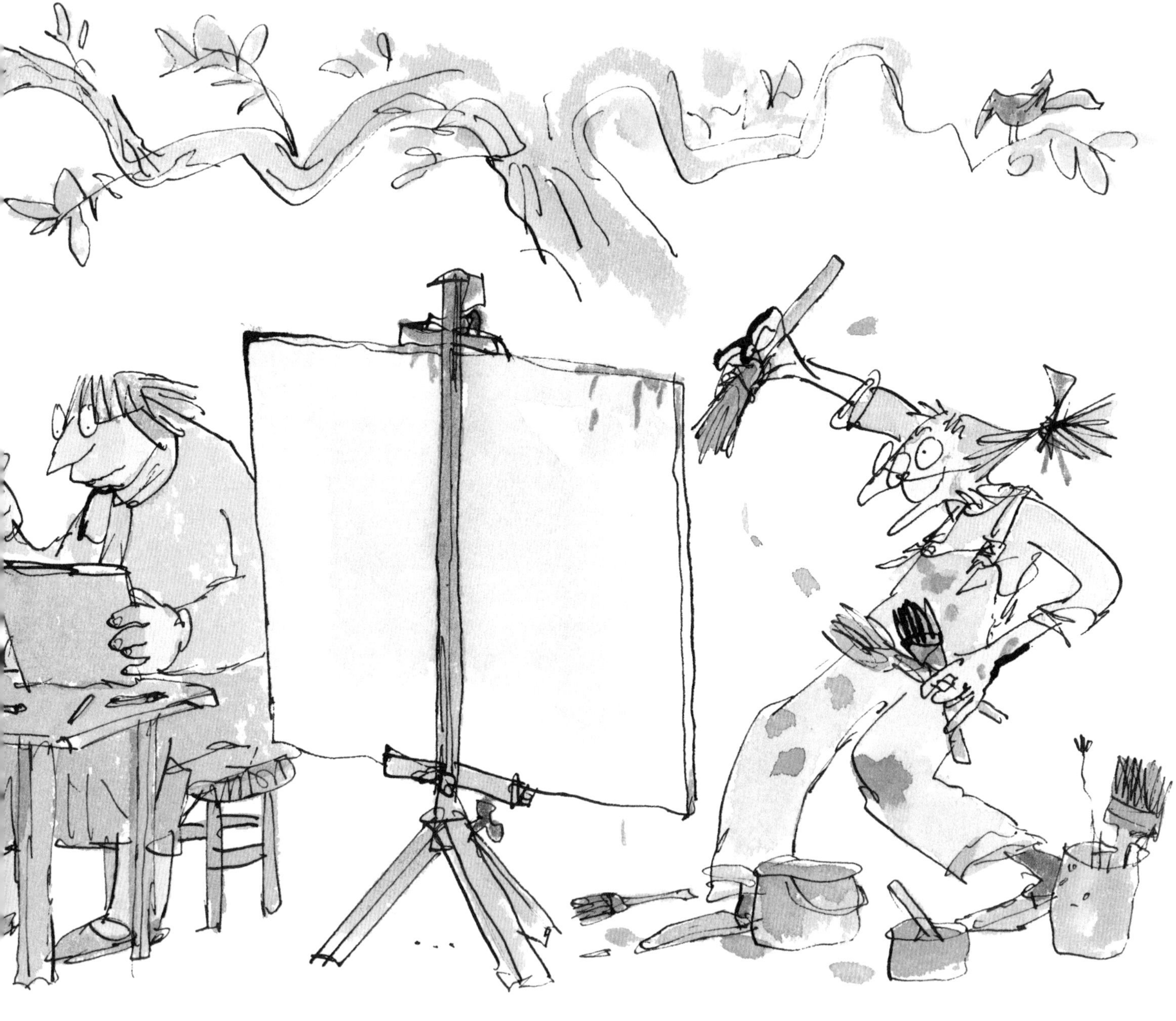

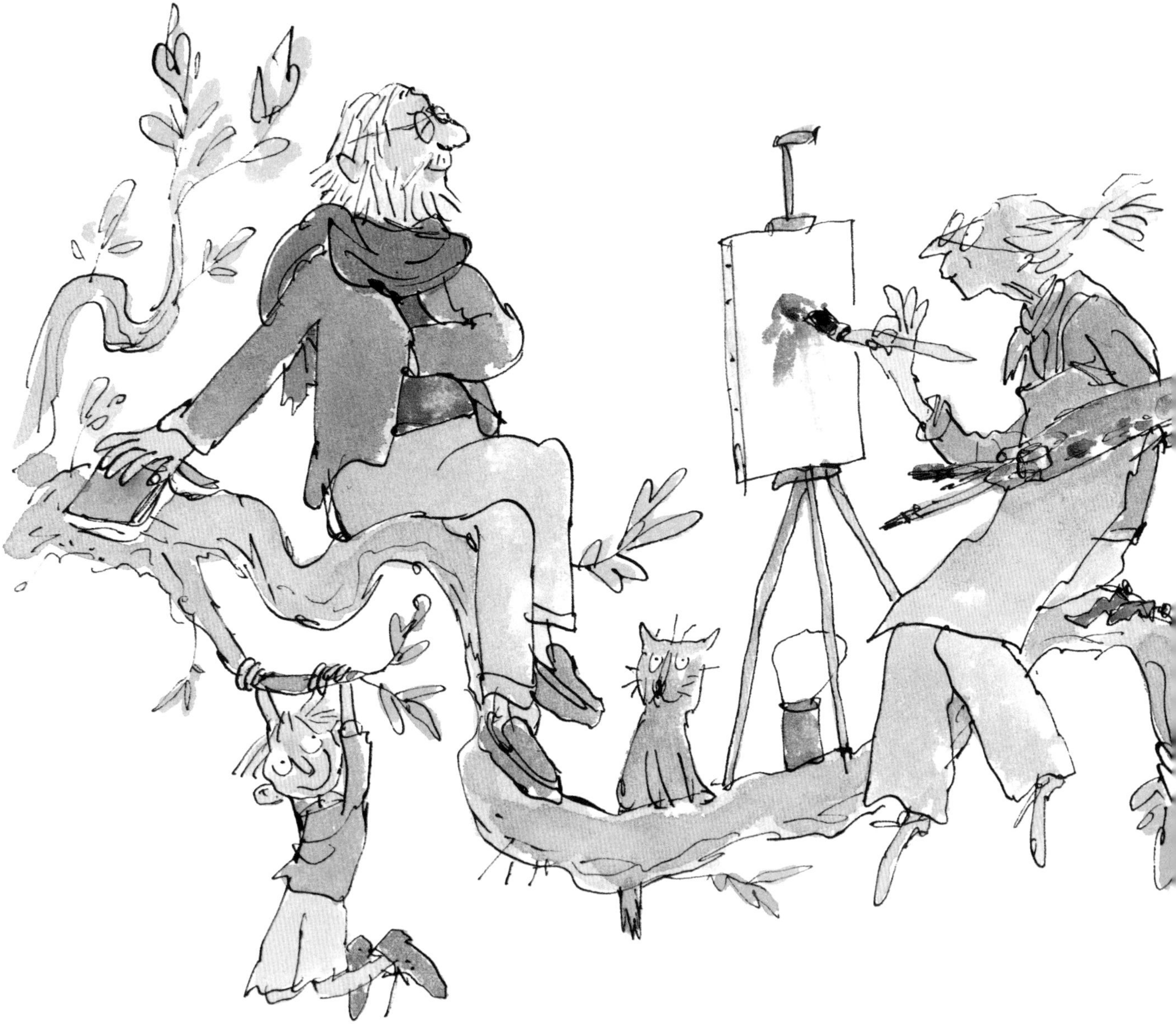

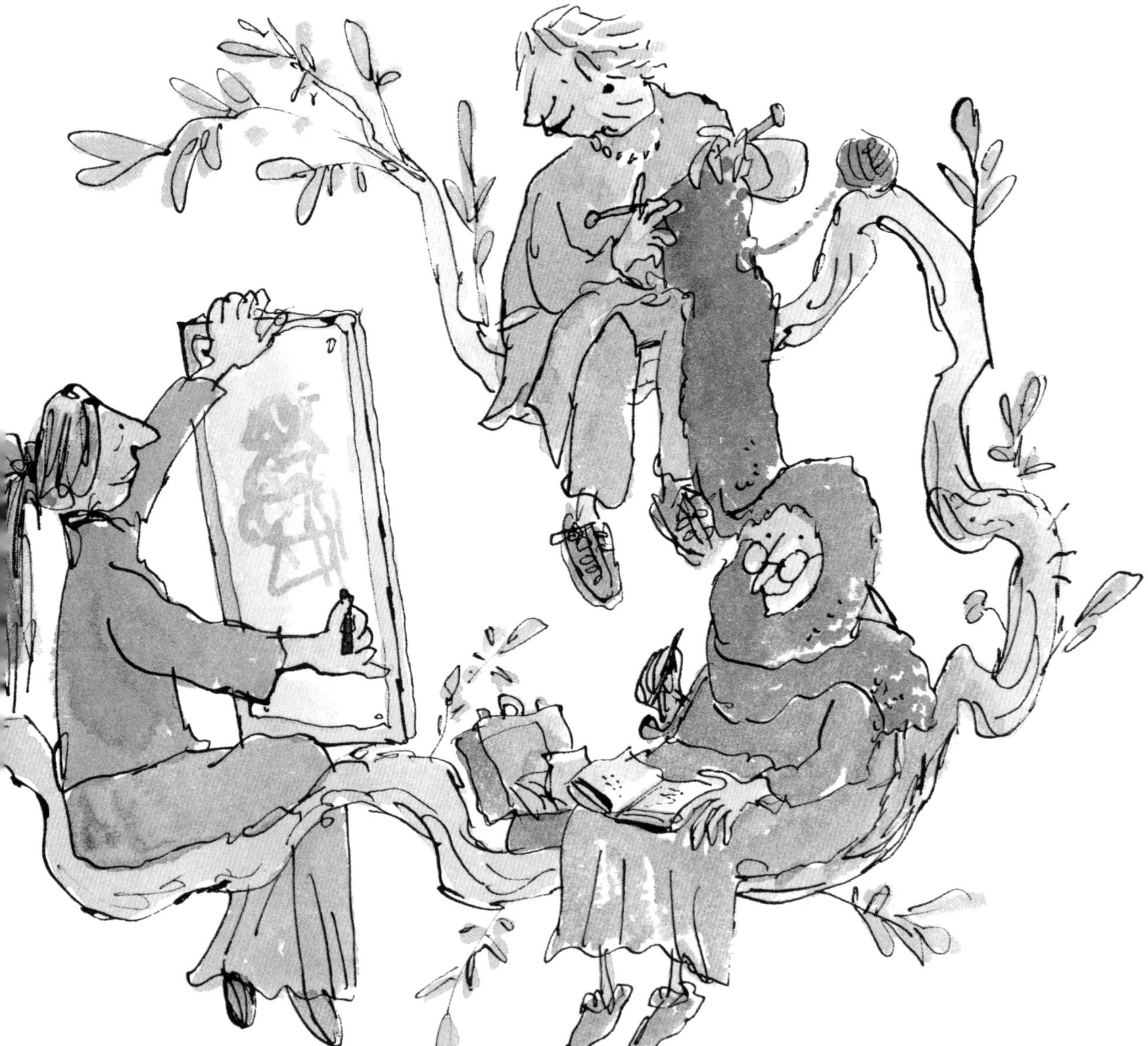

Special Occasions

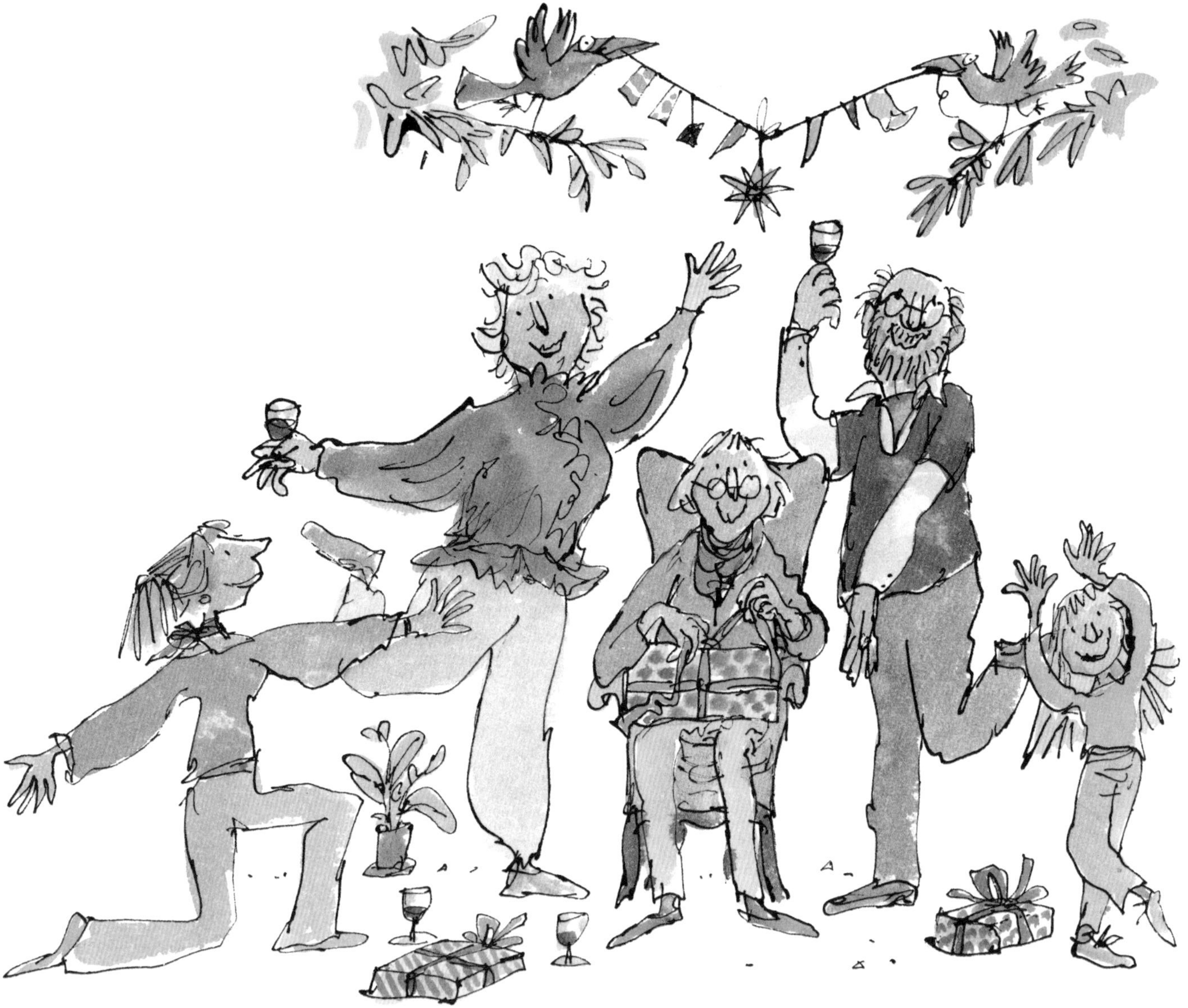

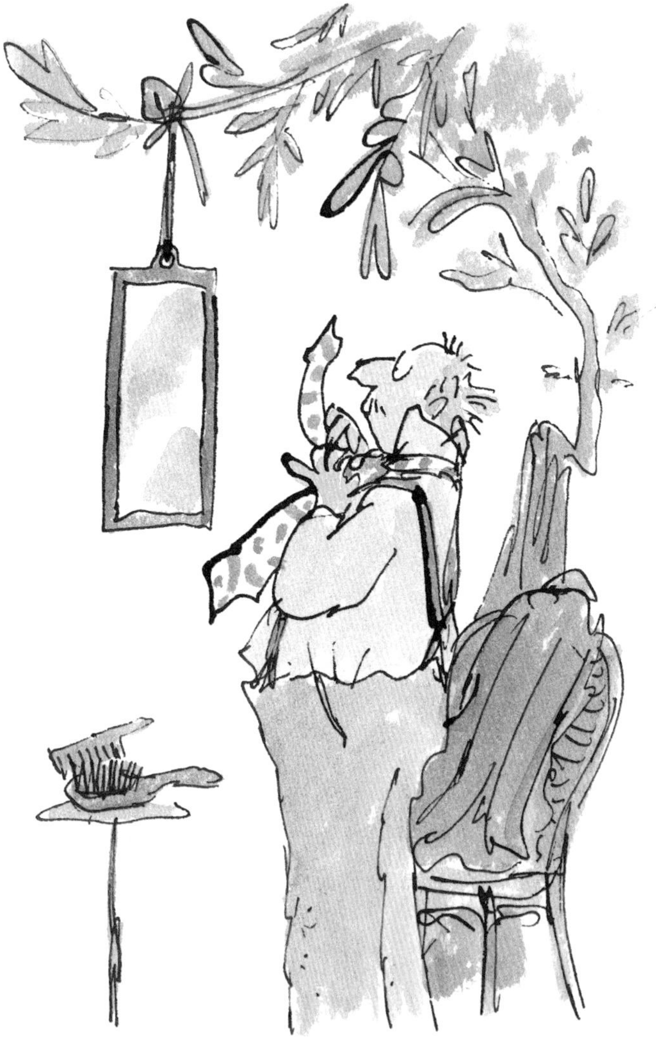

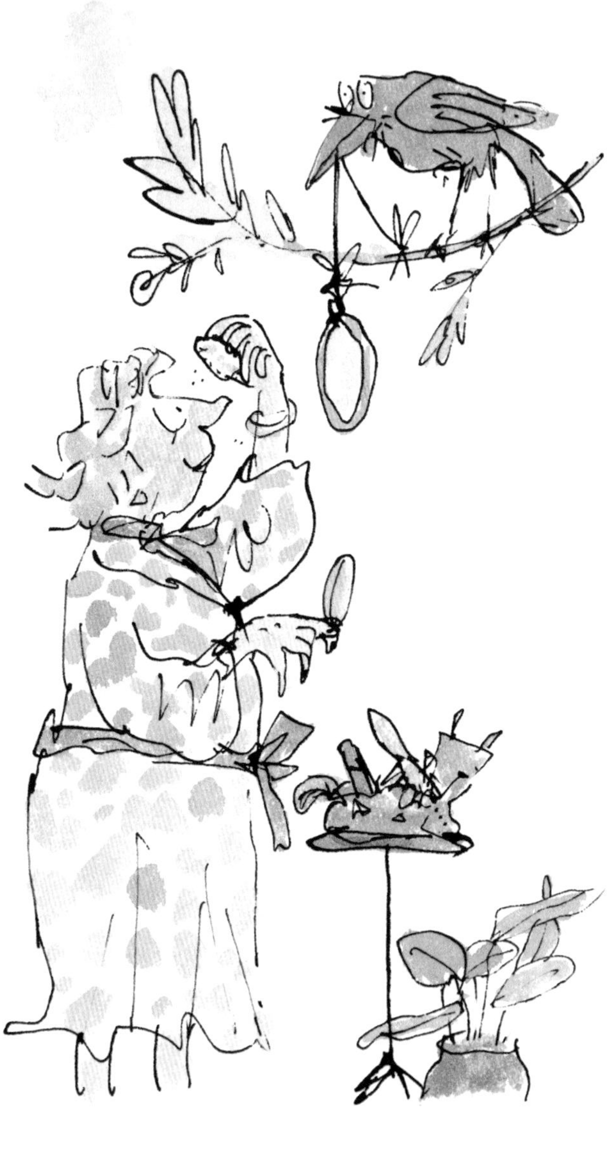

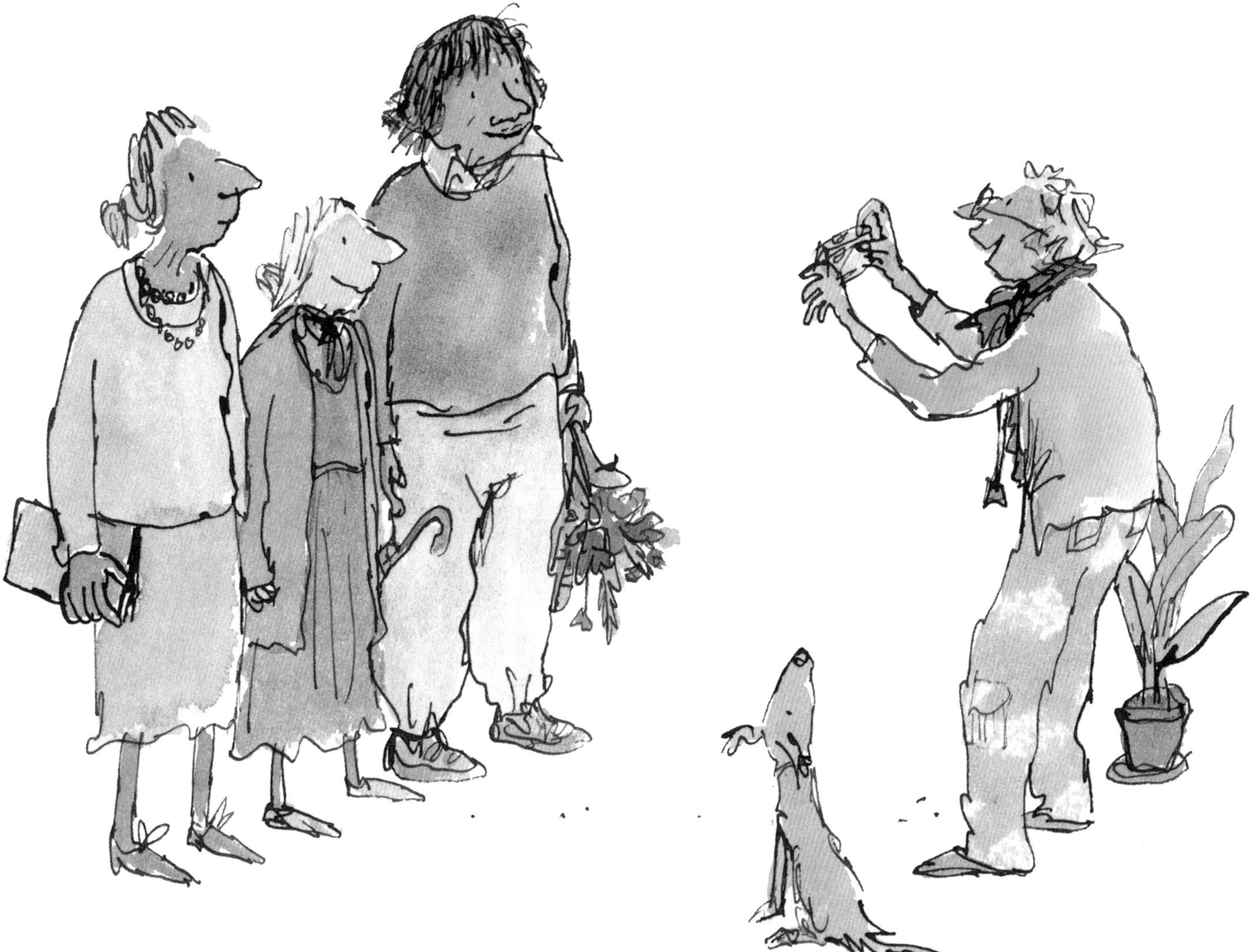

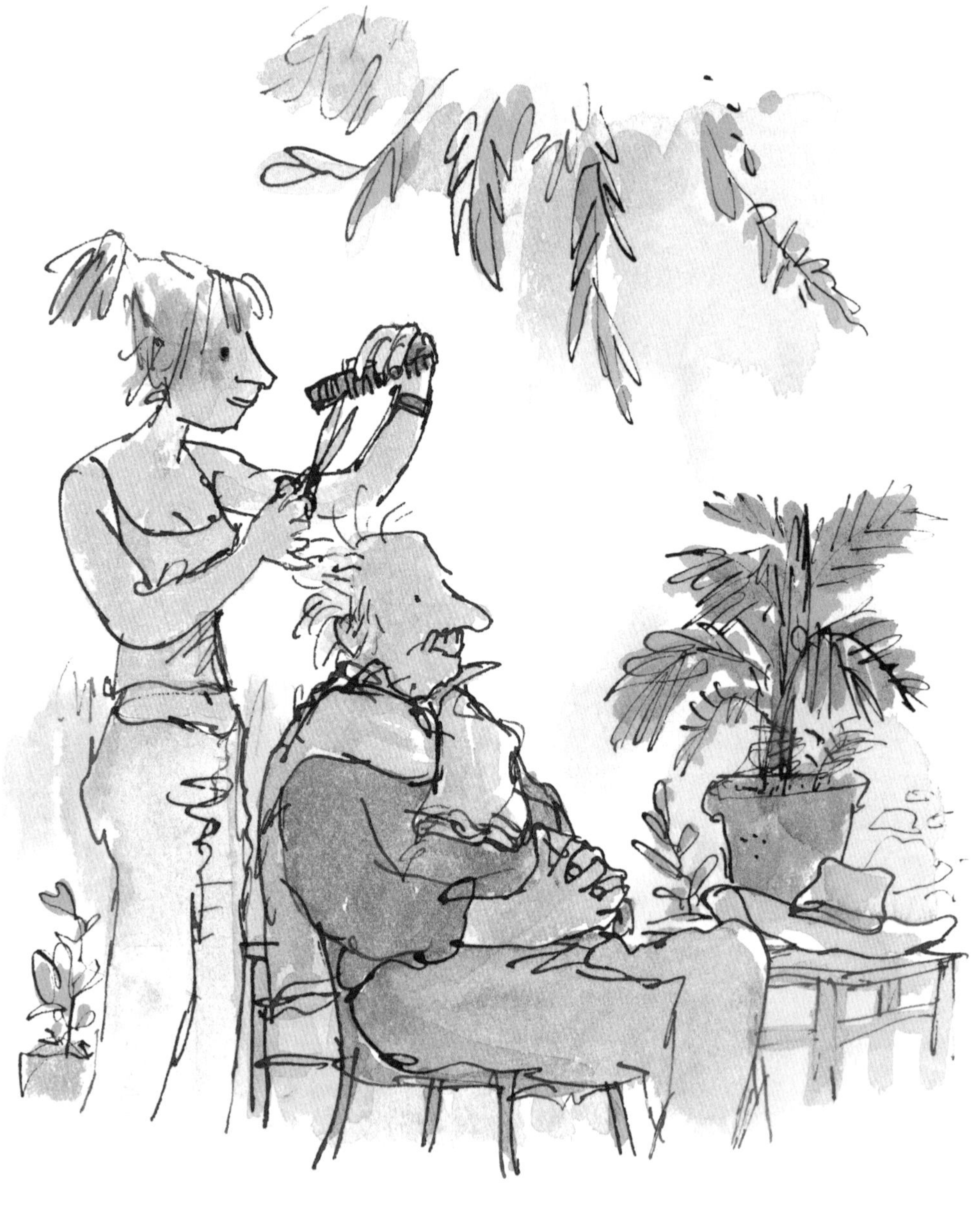

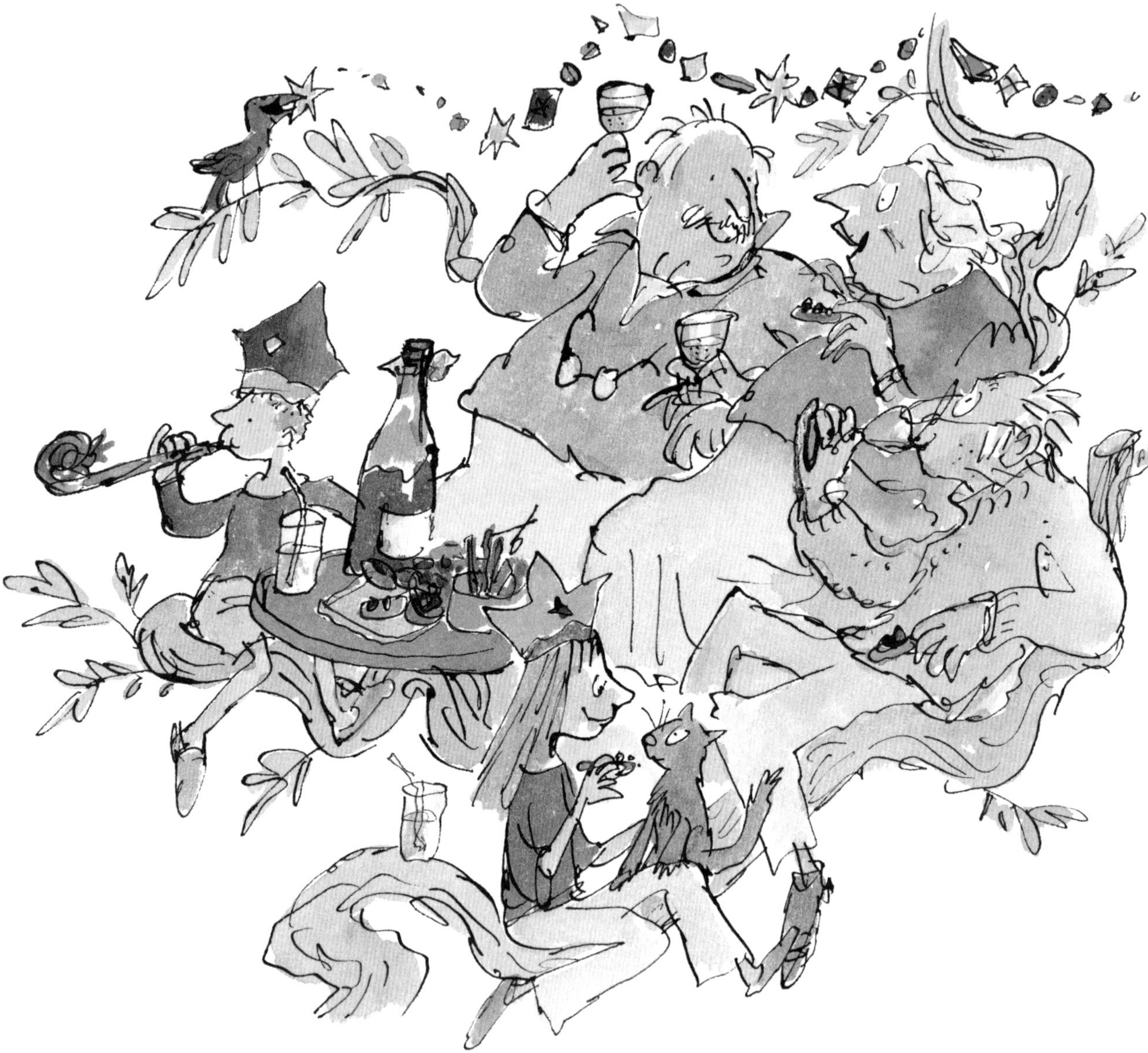

Looking back...

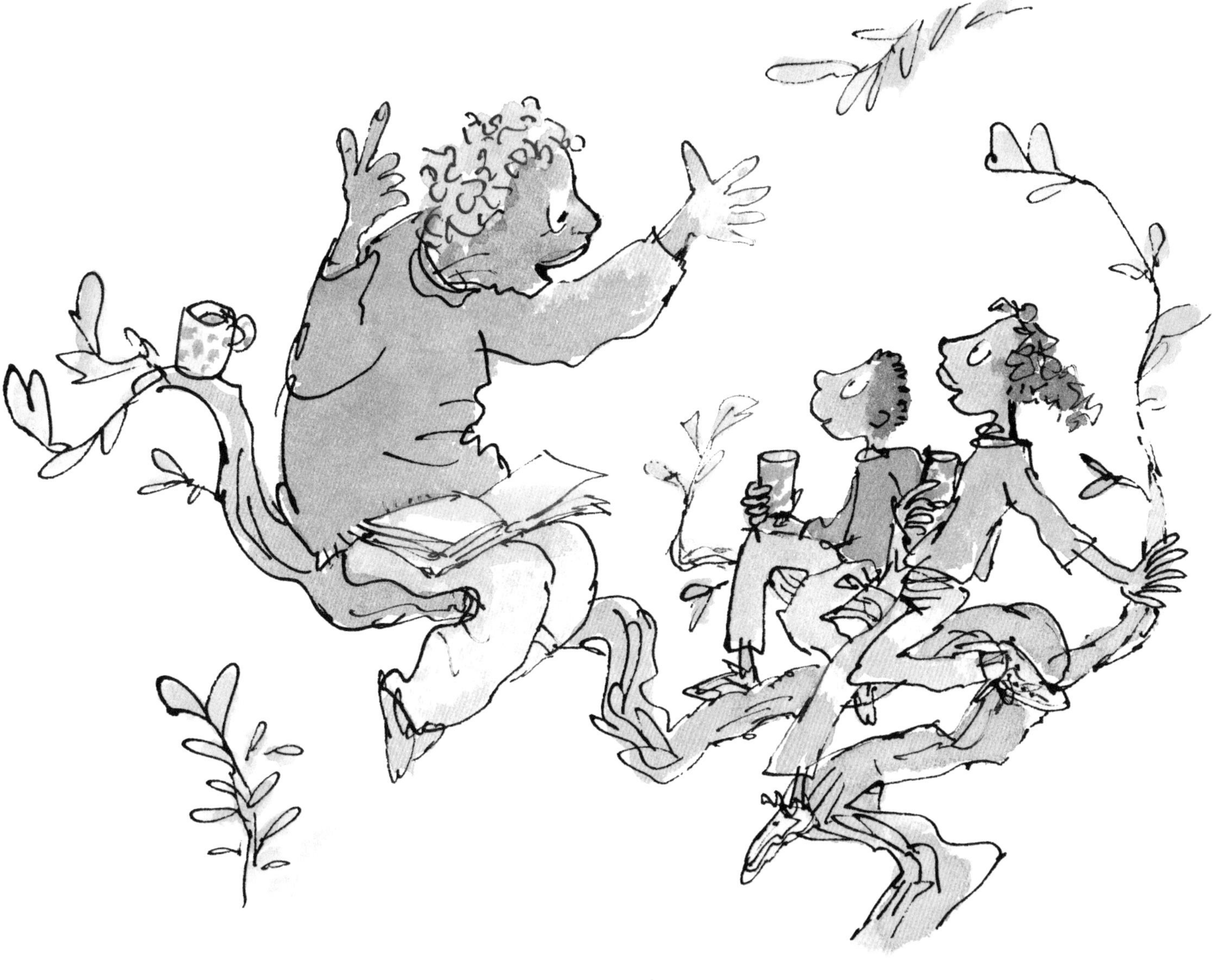

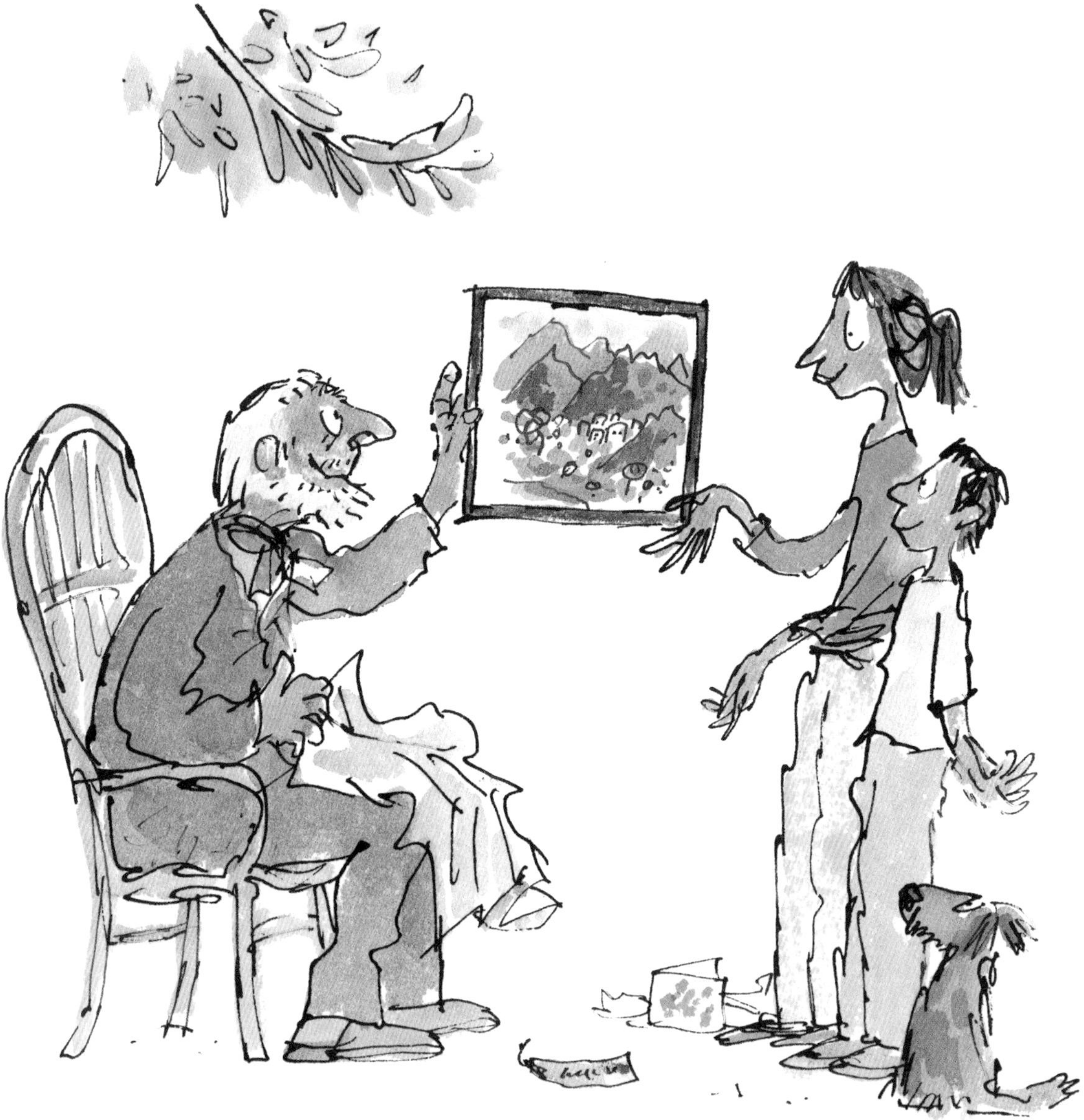

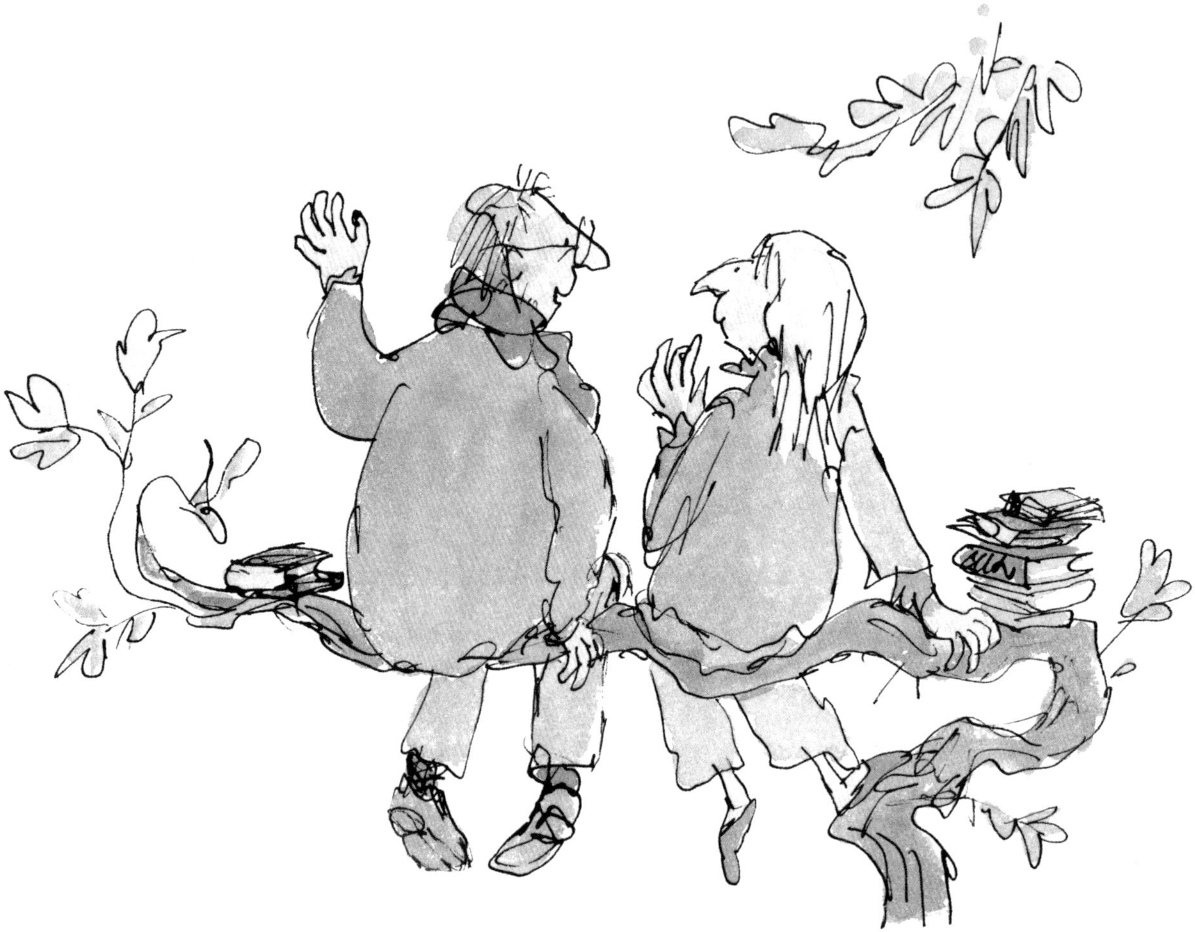